CW00728284

THE ILLUSTRATED DICTIONARY OF

INVENTORS and INVENTIONS

Copyright © 1994 Godfrey Cave Associates
First published 1994 in this format by
Bloomsbury Books
42 Bloomsbury Street
London WC1B 3QJ

Series editor: Merilyn Holme

Design: Jane Brett, Steven Hulbert
Illustrations: Jeremy Gower and Matthew White (B.L. Kearley);
Maltings Partnership; Oxford Illustrators; Jeremy Pyke; Simon Tegg.
Cover illustration: Jeremy Gower (B.L. Kearley Ltd)

Consultant: Peter Turvey, Member of Special Projects Group,
Science Museum, London.

Printed in Great Britain.

ISBN 1 85471 604 2

THE ILLUSTRATED DICTIONARY OF

INVENTORS and INVENTIONS

Contributors
Michael Pollard
Felicity Trotman
Merilyn Holme

Reader's notes

The entries in this dictionary have several features to help you understand more about the word you are looking up.

- Each entry is introduced by its headword. All the headwords in the dictionary are arranged in alphabetical order.

- Each headword is followed by a part of speech to show whether the word is used as a noun, adjective, verb or prefix.

- Each entry begins with a sentence that uses the headword as its subject.

- Words that are bold in an entry are cross references. You can look them up in this dictionary to find out more information about the topic.

- The sentence in italics at the end of an entry helps you to see how the headword can be used.

- Many of the entries are illustrated. The labels on the illustrations highlight all the key points of information.

- Many of the labels on the illustrations have their own entries in the dictionary and can therefore be used as cross references.

abacus *noun*

An abacus is a **calculating** machine. It is a framework on which wires strung with beads are stretched. Each bead stands for a number. An abacus is used by moving the beads to do calculations. Scientists think that the abacus may have been a **Mesopotamian invention** that first appeared around 3500 BC.
An expert can do sums with an abacus faster than with some electronic calculators.

Abu Ali al-Hasan ibn al-Haytham ► Alhazen

actinometer *noun*

An actinometer is a measuring instrument. It measures the heating power of the Sun's rays. The actinometer was invented by the British astronomer **Sir John Herschel** in 1825. It was built in 1856 by **Robert Bunsen** and Henry Roscoe.
Actinometers are now often called pyrheliometers.

adding machine *noun*

An adding machine is a **calculating** machine. It can add numbers up. The first successful adding machine with numbers marked on keys was made by D.E. Felt in 1887. When the keys were pressed, numbers were set down on paper. The sum was added up when a handle was pressed. Adding machines today are powered by electronic circuits.
Many shops and businesses use adding machines to help with their accounts.

aeolipyle *noun*

An aeolipyle was a very early form of **steam turbine**. Jets of steam were used to make a spherical **boiler** go round, or rotate. The aeolipyle was used as a toy, and was not developed at the time it was first made. It was invented by the Greek **Hero of Alexandria** who was born about AD 20.
The same idea used in the aeolipyle is used in a modern jet engine.

aerial ► antenna

aeroplane *noun*

An aeroplane is a kind of **aircraft**. It has fixed wings. An aeroplane is heavier than air. It uses a source of energy, such as a **jet engine**, to fly. The first aeroplane was made by the American brothers, **Wilbur and Orville Wright**. They made their first **flight** in this aeroplane in 1903. It was powered by a small petrol engine attached by chains to two **propellers**.
Since 1903, many kinds of aeroplane have been developed for military and civilian use.

aerosol can *noun*

An aerosol can is a metal can which sprays out liquid in a fine mist. Inside the can, a gas presses down on the liquid. When a push-button is pressed, the pressure of the gas forces the liquid out in tiny drops. Aerosol cans were invented by the Norwegian engineer Erik Rotheim in 1926. The idea was not used commercially until 1941.
Some modern aerosol cans use carbon dioxide gas to give pressure.

Aga *noun*

An Aga is a cooker. It contains a **furnace**, surrounded by a thick layer of metal. Coal can be burned in an Aga at a temperature of about 480 degrees Celsius. A thermostat controls the heat. This heat is used to cook food in ovens that can be hot enough to roast and bake, or cool enough to simmer food for a long time. On the top of the Aga are two or more boiling plates.

The Aga was invented by the Swedish scientist Dr Gustav Dalen in 1924.

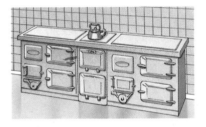

agricultural machinery ► page 8

air bed *noun*

An air bed is a **bed** or mattress made from a bag of air. It is made from two layers of cloth stuck to a thin sheet of rubber or plastic to make an airtight container. Air is pumped into the space between the cloth through a nozzle. The nozzle is shut with a cap to stop air escaping. When the air bed is no longer needed, the air can be let out.

The air bed was invented by John Clark, a grocer from Somerset in England, in 1813.

air brake *noun*

An air brake is a device that uses air under pressure to stop the movement of a **vehicle**. Air pressure is built up inside a tank with a **pump**. Then it is let out to stop the vehicle. Air brakes were invented by the American **George Westinghouse** for use on railways in 1867.

Air brakes are used on aeroplanes, lorries, railway engines and carriages.

air conditioning *noun*

Air conditioning is a way of controlling the temperature of an enclosed space. A space, such as a car or a building, must be sealed by having no open windows. Cooled or heated air is pumped into the space through ducts or pipes. Stale air is pumped away. The first air-conditioner was made by the American Willis H. Carrier in 1902.

Air conditioning allows people to work at comfortable temperatures.

air gun *noun*

An air gun is a **firearm**. It shoots by using air under pressure. Pulling the trigger causes air to compress, and this forces a bullet forwards. Some modern air guns use gases other than air, contained in special tanks. A very early form of air gun was built by Ctesibius of Alexandria between the years 170 and 161 BC. The first practical modern air gun was made in Germany in 1530.

Ctesibius's air gun was called a wind gun.

air pump *noun*

An air pump is a type of **pump**. It is used to suck air out of a container so that a vacuum is made. Vacuums made by air pumps were important in developing **X-rays** and **television** picture tubes. The German scientist **Otto von Guericke** invented the first successful air pump. In a public experiment in 1654, he pumped the air out of a copper sphere. The vacuum he made was so strong that 16 horses could not pull the two halves of the sphere apart.

Modern air pumps are usually powered by motor-driven pumps.

aircraft *noun*

An aircraft is a machine that flies in the air. Aircraft can have fixed wings, such as **aeroplanes** and **gliders**, or they can have rotating blades, such as **helicopters**. **Airships** and **balloons** can also be described as aircraft.

They saw many different kinds of aircraft in the exhibition about flying.

airship *noun*
An airship is a kind of **aircraft**. It is a **balloon** that can be steered by means of an **engine**. The gas that fills the balloon of an airship must be lighter than air. Early airships were often filled with hydrogen, but later designs used helium, which did not catch fire.
An airship was designed by the Italian Francesco de Lana in 1670. It was not until 1852 that the Frenchman Henri Giffard built an airship that flew.
The German Ferdinand von Zeppelin designed airships with rigid metal frames.

Alhazen (c. AD 965–1039)
Alhazen is the name used for the Arab scientist Abu Ali al-Hasan ibn al-Haytham. Alhazen was born in Basra but spent most of his life in Egypt. He was interested in light and colour, and how the eye sees. He explained how **lenses** work, and made **parabolic mirrors**.
Alhazen was the first person to suggest that rays of light pass from an object to the eye.

alphabet *noun*
An alphabet is a set of letters used in a language. The letters stand for sounds. An alphabet can also be a set of signs or symbols that stand for letters, such as the **morse code** or the **braille** alphabet. The first people to make use of an alphabet were the Phoenicians, in the years between 1700 and 1651 BC. Their alphabet had 22 letters.
The English alphabet contains 26 letters.

alternating current electric motor *noun*
An alternating current, or AC, electric motor is a **motor** powered by **electricity**. An alternating current of electricity can run in either direction. It is more efficient and economical in use than a direct current. The AC electric motor was invented by **Nikola Tesla**, working with **George Westinghouse**, in 1888.
Tesla's design for an AC electric motor is still in use today.

alternator *noun*
An alternator is an electric **generator**. It makes electrical energy in the form of an alternating current that changes its direction of flow many times a second. Modern power stations contain large alternators powered by **steam turbines**.
The alternator was invented by Hippolyte Pixii in 1831.

ambulance *noun*
An ambulance is a type of **vehicle**. It is used for taking sick or injured people to a hospital or a doctor for medical treatment. Most modern ambulances contain first-aid and other equipment for use in emergencies. They are operated by specially trained staff. The ambulance was invented in 1792 by the Frenchman Baron Dominique Jean Larrey.
Twelve fully-manned, horse-drawn ambulances went with every division of the army when Napoleon invaded Italy in 1796.

ambulance dating from 1812

agricultural machinery *noun*

Agricultural machinery is all the machines used in producing crops and rearing animals. The first agricultural machine to be invented was the **plough**, in about 7000 or 6000 BC. With the invention of the first mechanical **reaper** in 1826, the use of agricultural machinery became widespread.

The tractor is one of the most widely used items of agricultural machinery today.

The earliest known plough was made in the Near East in about 7000 or 6000 BC. It was simply a sharpened, forked branch that was drawn by people. By about 5000 BC, ploughs had been developed in the Middle East that could be pulled by oxen. A metal cap, called a share, was fitted to ploughs in Roman times, or about 1000 BC.

Egyptian wooden walking plough, 1300 BC

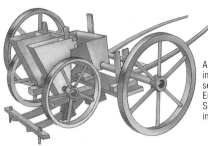

Jethro Tull's seed drill, 1700

A simple, hand-operated seed drill was first used in Sumeria in about 3000–2000 BC. A mechanical seed drill was invented in 1701 by Jethro Tull of England. It was the first modern farm machine. Some drills today place fertilizer as well as seeds in the soil.

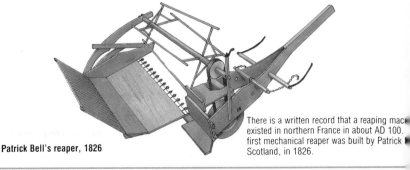

Patrick Bell's reaper, 1826

There is a written record that a reaping machine existed in northern France in about AD 100. first mechanical reaper was built by Patrick Scotland, in 1826.

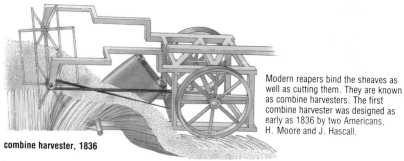

Modern reapers bind the sheaves as well as cutting them. They are known as combine harvesters. The first combine harvester was designed as early as 1836 by two Americans, H. Moore and J. Hascall.

combine harvester, 1836

In 1902 D. Albone of Great Britain invented the first successful petrol-driven tractor that was built in large numbers. It had three tyres made of steel, with ridges to allow the wheels to grip. Modern tractors are very powerful machines with huge, rubber tyres and up to 24 gears.

D. Albone's tractor, 1902

modern tractor

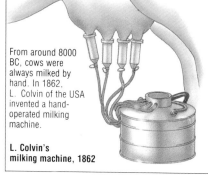

From around 8000 BC, cows were always milked by hand. In 1862, L. Colvin of the USA invented a hand-operated milking machine.

L. Colvin's milking machine, 1862

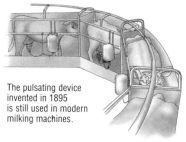

The pulsating device invented in 1895 is still used in modern milking machines.

modern milking machine

ammeter *noun*
An ammeter is an instrument used for measuring the strength of an electric current. There are two kinds of ammeter. Analogue ammeters have a dial with a needle that points to numbers. Digital ammeters are **electronic**. They have no moving parts. Ammeters were first used in 1879.
The scientist could see how strong the current was by reading the ammeter.

amplifier *noun*
An amplifier is a device that uses a source of energy to make a weak signal into a strong one. Modern amplifiers are usually electronic, making use of **transistors**. Several amplifiers may be joined together to make a signal strong enough to be heard. Amplifiers are used in machines such as **radios**, **microphones** and **televisions**.
The amplifier made the music so loud it could be heard across the fields.
amplify *verb*

Anacharsis the Scythian
Anacharsis was a Prince of Scythia, an ancient country in central Asia. Anacharsis travelled westwards to Greece in a search for knowledge. Here, he met many thinkers and scientists. He is said to have invented the **anchor**. Some scientists believe that he invented an anchor with flukes, between the years 600 and 591 BC.
Anacharsis the Scythian divided people into three kinds, the living, the dead and those who sail the sea in ships.

analytical engine *noun*
The analytical engine was a **calculating machine**. It could read mathematical problems from punched cards and then work out the answers. The analytical engine was designed by the Englishman **Charles Babbage** in the 1830s. Babbage's ideas were ahead of his time and the machine was never built.
The analytical engine would have been an early form of computer.

anchor *noun*
An anchor is a heavy device that holds a **ship** or a **balloon** in place. In early times, anchors of wood or metal were made with flukes. Flukes were metal plates shaped like triangles that stuck out from the body of the anchor. They dug into the sea-bed, holding the ship more securely. Some scientists believe that **Anacharsis the Scythian** invented the anchor with flukes.
In very early times, anchors were large stones, attached to ships by ropes.

baskets of stones served as anchors

anemometer *noun*
An anemometer is an instrument for measuring. It measures the speed of the wind. In a mechanical anemometer, the moving air spins a vertical rod with cups on the top. A hot-wire anemometer measures how quickly the wind cools a wire heated by electricity. An early anemometer was invented in 1709 by Wolfius.
The cup anemometer was invented in 1846 by Thomas R. Robinson, an Irish scientist.

aneroid barometer *noun*
An aneroid barometer is an instrument that measures air pressure. It contains a metal box with a vacuum inside. Small changes in air pressure cause the sides of the box to change shape. An early aneroid barometer was invented by Zaiker in 1758. The first modern aneroid barometer was invented by the Frenchman Lucien Vidi in 1843.
Most barometers in homes are aneroid barometers.

antenna (plural **antennae**)   *noun*
An antenna is a device for sending and receiving **radio** and other electromagnetic signals. Radio and **television** sets have antennae to receive signals. The German Heinrich Hertz first used an antenna to send out radio signals in 1885. One of the most familiar modern antennae is the yagi antenna. This was invented by the Japanese Hidetsugu Yagi, who **patented** it in 1926.
Many homes use yagi antennae to receive television signals.

Appert, Nicolas (1749–1841)
Nicolas Appert lived in Paris. He worked as a cook. Appert was interested in ways of keeping food. He tried heating food in sealed glass containers, becoming the first person to bottle food. For his invention, Nicolas Appert was given 12,000 francs by Napoleon. Bottled food was easy to carry about, and kept fresh for a long time. Appert also invented the bouillon cube.
The modern food preservation industry began with the work of Nicolas Appert.

aqualung   *noun*
An aqualung is a device that allows a diver to breathe under water. Air under pressure is carried in one or more tanks on the back of the diver. The air flows along a pipe and through a **valve** to the diver's mouth.
The modern aqualung was invented in 1943 by the Frenchmen Jacques-Yves Cousteau and Emile Gagnan.

aqueduct   *noun*
An aqueduct is a structure for moving water from one place to another. It can be a **bridge** that carries a water channel. It can also be a system of **canals**, tunnels and bridges that supply water. Early aqueducts used gravity to make the water flow. King Sennacherib of Assyria built the earliest known aqueduct in 700 BC. It was 48 kilometres long.
The Romans built large aqueduct systems to bring water to their cities.

Arab invention   *noun*
Arab invention describes the machines and ideas that came from the Arab peoples of the Arabian peninsula and North Africa. From the AD 600s, Arab scholars worked out laws of mathematics and medicine. They made inventions and improvements in areas such as **irrigation**, **windmill** design and the making of **ceramics**, **glass** and **paper**.
The rich cloth woven first in Damascus and called damask was an Arab invention.

arc light   *noun*
An arc light is a kind of **lamp**. It gives a very bright light. The light is made by a spark of **electricity** that jumps between two carbon rods. Arc lights are used when very brilliant light is needed, such as in **lighthouses**. The arc light was invented by the English scientist **Sir Humphry Davy** in 1805.
The first arc lights produced a great deal of smoke and heat.

Archimedean screw   *noun*
An Archimedean screw is a device that is used for **irrigation**. It is a spiral **screw** that turns in a cylinder by means of a handle. As the handle is turned, water is carried up the screw from a river. When it reaches the top of the screw, the water falls into a container. Archimedean screws are said to have been invented by the Greek scientist **Archimedes**.
The Archimedean screw is a very efficient way of using energy to move water.

Archimedes   (c. 287–212 BC)
Archimedes was a Greek scientist, born in Syracuse in Sicily. He studied in Alexandria, and made many discoveries in mathematics, mechanics and engineering. Archimedes discovered how **levers** work. He is said to have moved a fully-laden warship by himself to demonstrate his ideas about levers. Archimedes also invented a kind of **pulley**, and many weapons, such as **cranes** and **catapults**.
Some scientists think Archimedes invented the Archimedean screw.

Argand burner   *noun*
An Argand burner was an oil **lamp**. An Argand burner had a cylindrical wick so that oil could reach both sides of the flame. This gave better light. The ideas used for the Argand burner were used later for **gas lamps**.
The Argand burner was made by the Swiss Aimé Argand, and patented in 1784.

armour   ▶   arms and armour

armoured vehicle   *noun*
An armoured vehicle is a **vehicle** that is protected from attack by enemies. Thick metal plates are used to protect vehicles such as cars, trains and ships that may be used in war. The first armoured ship was invented by the Korean **Admiral Yi-sun-Sin** during a war against the Japanese.
The tank was designed as an armoured vehicle during the First World War.

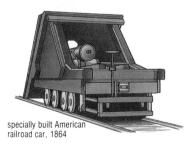

specially built American railroad car, 1864

arms and armour   ▶   page 14

artificial heart   *noun*
An artificial heart is a **machine**. It is used to replace a natural heart when the natural heart is too badly diseased to work properly. An artificial heart contains two **pumps**. One pumps blood to the lungs, and the other pumps blood to other organs in the body.
The artificial heart was invented by the Dutchman Willem Kolff in 1957.

artificial kidney   *noun*
An artificial kidney is a **machine**. It is used when the real kidneys are diseased, or have been removed. An artificial kidney can wash waste products out of the blood, and return clean blood to a patient's body. The artificial kidney was invented by the Dutchman Dr Willem J. Kolff in 1944.
An artificial kidney can also be called a renal dialysis machine.

artificial limb   *noun*

An artificial limb is a device that can replace a human limb. Artificial limbs are used to help people who have lost limbs through illness or accident. The Ancient Greeks were the first to use artificial limbs. The modern use of artificial limbs dates from 1540, when the French surgeon **Ambrose Paré** invented mechanical limbs using hinges, levers and cog-wheels.
Modern artificial limbs are made with carbon fibre, using computers.

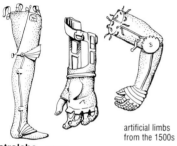

artificial limbs
from the 1500s

astrolabe   *noun*

An astrolabe is an instrument used in navigation and in astronomy. Astrolabes were used to find out the position of a star or other heavenly body, or the position of a ship at sea. The astrolabe was invented by the Greek Hipparchus of Rhodes in 130 BC.
Modern navigators use instruments such as compasses, as they are more accurate than the astrolabe.

astronomical clock   *noun*

An astronomical clock is a kind of **clock**. It shows the movements of the stars and planets, and gives details of the phases of the Moon. An astronomical clock may also give details of the time it takes the Earth to rotate past the stars. Some scientists think that Stonehenge in Britain, built around 2000 BC, was used as an astronomical clock.
The first mechanical astronomical clock was made by the Chinese Su Sung in 1092.

astronomical telescope ► telescope

atomic clock   *noun*

An atomic clock is a kind of **clock**. It measures time. Atomic clocks are very accurate. They can lose as little time as one second every three million years. Atomic clocks are very important for scientists, such as astronomers, who need accurate **timekeeping**. The first atomic clock was invented in 1948, by the American Dr Willard Frank Libby.
Atomic clocks are used as standards for setting international time.

automatic telephone exchange   *noun*

An automatic telephone exchange is a connecting point for **telephone** calls. When telephones were first invented, calls were connected by hand. The first automatic telephone exchanges used **electricity** to work machinery that could make connections without operators. Modern automatic telephone exchanges use electronic switchboards.
The automatic telephone exchange was invented in 1889 by the American Almon Brown Strowger.

automobile ► motor car

axle   *noun*

An axle is the rod or shaft to which a **wheel** is attached. Some early axles were fixed to the wheel, and turned with it. Later axles were fixed to a **vehicle** or machine in such a way that the wheel turned separately. The first axles were used with the first wheeled vehicles in Sumeria, in the years between 3500 and 3000 BC.
Modern vehicles may have one axle for many wheels.

arms and armour   *noun*

Arms and armour are the weapons and the defence against weapons that people have used for thousands of years. In prehistoric times, people made spears and arrowheads from sharpened flint stones. They protected themselves with simple, leather armour. Modern weapons can kill thousands of people in one go. Special vests can stop a bullet.

Arms and armour have always played an important part in the forming of the world's civilizations.

Attack

30,000 BC — bow and arrow

1.5 million BC — flint weapons

3500 BC — Bronze Age sw

Defence

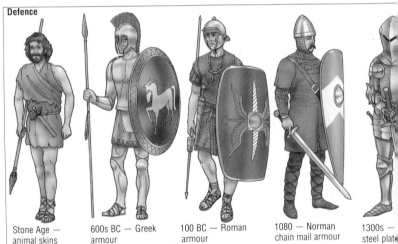

Stone Age — animal skins

600s BC — Greek armour

100 BC — Roman armour

1080 — Norman chain mail armour

1300s — steel plate

400 BC — giant catapult

1320 — pot-de-fer cannon of Europe

1400 — hand cannon, the first gun

1100 — European crossbow

1945 — atomic bomb

1500 — Japanese samurai armour

1600s — armour with steel plates

1914–18 — 1st World War

Military clothing of today

Babbage, Charles (1791–1871)

Charles Babbage was born in London, and became a professor of mathematics at Cambridge University. He wanted to stop the mistakes that happened when mathematical calculations were made by hand. In 1821, he invented and tried to build the **difference engine**. He gave this project up after an argument with his colleague. From 1834 to 1854, he worked on the **analytical engine**.
Charles Babbage's ideas were far ahead of his time.

Babylonian invention ►
Mesopotamian invention

Baird, John Logie (1886–1946)

John Logie Baird was a Scottish pioneer of **television**. He spent many years trying to send pictures using **radio** waves. In 1924, he succeeded in sending an image several feet. Baird made his success public in 1926, and the British Broadcasting Corporation used his method for some years.
The first television set built by John Logie Baird included a biscuit tin, a tea chest and darning needles.

ball-bearings noun

Ball-bearings are a part of some **machines**. They are small steel balls that help to reduce the friction caused when moving parts rub together. The moving parts are often rods or shafts that turn, such as the pedals of a **bicycle**. Ball-bearings support the turning rod, rolling as the rod moves.
Ball-bearings were made by the Italian goldsmith Benvenuto Cellini in 1543.

balloon noun

A balloon is a kind of **aircraft**. It is lighter than air, and cannot be steered. Balloons are made from a large, round bag, or envelope, attached by ropes to a basket. A balloon's envelope can be filled with light gas, such as hydrogen or helium, or with hot air. The first important balloon flights were made by Joseph-Michel and Jacques Etienne Montgolfier. These flights began in 1783.
A small hot-air balloon is said to have been used in Portugal in 1709.

ballpoint pen noun

A ballpoint pen is a type of **writing** instrument. It has a turning ball instead of a nib, that delivers **ink**. The first ballpoint pen was designed to work on a rough surface, such as canvas. The invention was **patented** by the American John H. Loud in 1888. It was never used, but the idea was taken up later by the Hungarian Lazlo Biro. Biro developed his pen in Argentina, and patented it in 1938. He filled his pen with the quick-drying ink used by printers.
Biro's ballpoint pen was sold to a French company, BiC, and is now used world-wide.

bandsaw noun

A bandsaw is a kind of cutting tool. It is a **saw** with an endless blade. The blade runs over wheels. Modern bandsaws are usually powered by **electricity**. The bandsaw was invented by the Englishman William Newberry in 1808.
The bandsaw was not much used until 1850, when better steel allowed a blade to be made that did not snap easily.

bank *noun*
A bank is a place where business to do with
money is carried out. Banks can deal with
money for governments, companies or
individual people. Banks seem to have been
a **Mesopotamian invention**. Lists of money
dealings have been found on clay tablets
dating from around 2500 BC. Early modern
banks developed in Italy in the AD 800s.
Many people keep their money in banks.

banknote *noun*
A banknote is a promise. It is a piece of
paper on which a bank has written a promise
to pay the owner a certain amount of **money**.
A banknote is light and easy to carry, so it is
often used instead of money in the form of
metal **coins**. Banknotes were a **Chinese
invention**. They were in use in the years
between AD 880 and 910.
*Modern banknotes were invented by
Johannes Palmerstuck of Sweden in 1658.*

Chinese banknote from the 1300s

banknote numbering machine *noun*
A banknote numbering machine is a
security device. It makes it more difficult to
forge **banknotes**. As banknotes are printed,
the banknote numbering machine prints a
number on each note. Banks can keep
records of the numbered banknotes. The
banknote numbering machine was invented
by the Englishman **Joseph Bramah** in 1806.
*When the Bank of England first started to
use a banknote numbering machine,
100 employees lost their jobs.*

bar code *noun*
A bar code is a kind of message that can be
read by a **computer**. It is a pattern of lines
and spaces. The lines and spaces make up
a coded message, such as a price. Bar
codes can be read by **lasers** that are part of
a computerized **cash register** in a shop. Bar
codes were invented in 1970, by Monarch
Markings in the United States of America,
and Plessey Telecommunications Ltd in
England.
*The full name for a bar code is a computer-
scanned binary signal code.*

barometer *noun*
A barometer is an instrument for measuring
the pressure of the atmosphere. There are
two kinds of barometer, the **aneroid
barometer** and the mercury **barometer**.
In a mercury barometer, changes in
atmospheric pressure force mercury up
a tube. The higher the mercury, the
stronger the pressure. The mercury
barometer was invented in 1643 by the
Italian Evangelista Torricelli.
*Torricelli based his barometer on an idea he
had been given by Galileo.*

bath *noun*
A bath is a kind of tank in which a body can
be covered in water. Baths are mostly used
for washing, but they can also be used for
medical treatments. Baths need a good
supply of water. Some need a supply of
energy to heat the water. The first bathroom
with a bath and a water supply was built at
the palace of Knossos on Crete, between
2000 and 1950 BC.
The Romans built baths in many towns.

Queen's bath, Knossos, Crete

17

bathyscaphe *noun*
A bathyscaphe is a **vehicle** designed to go deep down into the sea. It is powered by **electricity**, and passengers can see out through a special plastic window. The bathyscaphe was invented by the Swiss scientist August Piccard in 1960.
A bathyscaphe was used for a record descent of 10,900 metres into the sea.

battery *noun*
A battery is a device for turning chemical energy into electrical energy. Some batteries are disposable. This means that when they run down, they are thrown away. Other batteries are rechargeable. This means they can be recharged with **electricity** and used again. The battery was invented by the Italian **Alessandro Volta** in 1800.
Rechargeable batteries are used in cars and lorries.

bayonet

bayonet *noun*
A bayonet is a blade. It can be attached to the barrel of a **firearm**, such as a rifle. Bayonets are used by soldiers when fighting hand-to-hand. The first bayonets plugged into the barrel of a **musket**. More modern designs are attached by rings or clips. The bayonet was invented in 1590 in the town of Bayonne, in France. It was widely used as a weapon towards the end of the 1600s.
Bayonets are weapons used for stabbing.

bazooka *noun*
A bazooka is a weapon. It is made up of a thin metal tube, through which a **rocket** is launched. The rocket has an explosive head and can damage **armoured vehicles**.
The bazooka was invented in 1939 by the Swiss Mohaupt brothers.

Beaufort Scale *noun*
The Beaufort Scale is a measurement. It is used to measure the force of the wind. Winds are graded on a scale from 0, calm, to 12, hurricane. The Beaufort Scale is easy to use because it depends on seeing signs, such as smoke rising or trees moving. It was invented in 1805 by an English seaman, Sir Francis Beaufort.
The Beaufort Scale has now been increased to 17, to record wind speed accurately.

bed *noun*
A bed is a piece of furniture. It is used for rest or sleep. A bed is a framework of wood or metal, that supports a mattress on ropes or springs. The mattress is a bag of cloth stuffed with a soft material, such as feathers. The earliest known beds were in common use in Ancient Egypt around 2500 BC.
Modern beds include air beds and water beds.

Bell, Alexander Graham (1847–1922)
Alexander Graham Bell was born in Edinburgh, and educated at Edinburgh and London universities. He taught deaf people, and was interested in ways of making and sending out sounds. In 1873, he became a professor at Boston University in the United States of America In 1876, Bell invented the **telephone**. He also improved the **gramophone** and designed a giant **kite**.
Alexander Graham Bell was a founder of the 'National Geographic' Magazine.

bellows *plural noun*
A bellows is a **machine** that forces air in a particular direction. Air is sucked into a bag of heavy material, such as leather. Then it is pumped out again. Bellows work when handles are pulled and pushed. Bellows are often used to pump air at a fire to keep it burning hotly. Bellows were used in the making of **glass** and metals from 1600 BC.
Between 310 and 300 BC, the Chinese invented a bellows that blew air in a continuous stream.

belt drive   *noun*

A belt drive is a way of moving energy from one place to another. It is an endless belt that connects two shafts. A source of energy moves the belt, and in turn the belt moves the shafts. Belts can be flat or V-shaped. The Chinese Yang Hsiung described a belt drive in his book, 'Dictionary of Local Expressions', in 11 BC. The belt drive was not known in Europe until 1430.

A car's alternator is a well-known belt drive.

Benz, Carl Friedrich (1844–1929)

Carl Benz was born in Karlsruhe in Germany. He learned engineering in factories, and became interested in the **internal combustion engine**. In 1885, Benz invented a three-wheeled **motor car**. It had an internal combustion engine cooled with water. The car drove at a top speed of 24 kilometres an hour. By 1890, Benz had designed a more powerful, four-wheeled car.

Carl Benz invented the first practical car.

Berliner, Emile (1851–1929)

Emile Berliner was born in Hanover, Germany, but emigrated to the United States of America. He became interested in sound **recording** and, in 1887, invented the **gramophone**. The machine played a **gramophone record**, that was also invented by Berliner.

The gramophone record invented by Emile Berliner has allowed many people to enjoy listening to music.

Bessemer, Sir Henry (1813–1898)

Henry Bessemer was born in Charlton in England. He was interested in metals, and tried to find a form of iron that would be strong enough for a rifled **gun barrel** he had invented. In his search for this iron, he invented the **bessemer converter**, a way of making steel cheaply. In 1840, Henry Bessemer helped invent the first **type-composing machine**.

When he died, Sir Henry Bessemer had taken out patents on 114 inventions.

bessemer converter   *noun*

A bessemer converter is a container in which steel can be made cheaply for **metalworking**. In a bessemer converter, air is blown through molten iron. Unwanted carbon combines with the air and burns away. The process generates heat so that the iron can then be turned into steel without using any more fuel.

The bessemer converter was invented by Sir Henry Bessemer in 1856.

bicycle   *noun*

A bicycle is a **vehicle**. It has a metal frame with two **wheels**, one behind the other. The wheels move when a person pushes two pedals round. The first bicycle with pedals was invented by the Scot Kirkpatrick Macmillan in 1839. The first modern bicycle was built in 1885 by John Starley.

By 1890, rubber tyres filled with air were used for bicycles.

bifocal lens *noun*
A bifocal lens is an **optical invention**. It is a type of **lens** that has two focal points. Light rays that pass through it meet at two different points. The top focal point allows the eye to see objects at a distance. The bottom focal point allows the eye to see objects close up. The bifocal lens was invented by the American **Benjamin Franklin** in 1784.
Many people wear spectacles with bifocal lenses.

Birdseye, Clarence (1886–1956)
Clarence Birdseye was born in New York. In 1916, he made a journey to Labrador in Canada. On the journey, he found that fish that had been frozen quickly tasted very good when it had been thawed and cooked. Birdseye developed ways of freezing food fast. In 1924, he set up the General Seafoods Company to sell frozen food.
When he died, Clarence Birdseye had taken out about 300 patents for his inventions.

biro ► **ballpoint pen**

blast furnace *noun*
A blast furnace is a container in which iron ore is smelted to make iron. It is filled up with iron ore, coke and limestone. Hot air is forced into the mixture. This burns the coke and melts the iron in the ore. As the iron melts, it runs to the bottom of the blast furnace. The blast furnace was a **Chinese invention** of the AD 500s.
Early European blast furnaces were built in Scandinavian countries in about AD 800.

bleaching powder *noun*
Bleaching powder is a chemical. It is a kind of bleach that takes the colour out of materials and makes them whiter. Bleaches are used to make **paper** and textiles. They are also used in homes. Until bleaching powder was invented, bleaches were liquid. Powder is easier to handle than liquid. It was invented in 1799 by the British chemical manufacturer, Charles Tennant.
Bleaching powder is a mixture of chlorine and slaked lime, or calcium hydroxide.

boiler *noun*
A boiler is a container in which water is turned into steam. Steam is produced by heating the water. Boilers can be small, such as those used for **central heating** in homes. Large boilers are used to make steam for power stations. Boilers were very important for the development of **steam engines**. The Frenchman **Denis Papin** invented the first boiler with a safety valve, in about 1670.
A kettle is a well-known form of boiler.

bomb *noun*
A bomb is a device designed to explode. It can be thrown, placed in position, or dropped from an aircraft. Bombs were a **Chinese invention**, and were in use by the year 1221. These bombs were filled with **gunpowder** and pieces of metal, or shrapnel. Today, there are many different kinds of bomb, such as incendiary bombs, guided bombs and nuclear bombs.
Hydrogen bombs are the most powerful.

Chinese bomb with fuse from the 1600s

20

book *noun*
A book is a set of sheets, made of a material such as **paper**, and covered in **written** or **printed** words. The sheets are folded and bound into a cover. Books are used to store and carry about information. Books written by hand on papyrus scrolls were made in Egypt around 2700 BC. The oldest known printed book is Chinese. It is the 'Diamond Sutra' of AD 868.
Johannes Gutenberg of Germany printed books from moveable type from 1453.

bow and arrow *noun*
A bow and arrow is a weapon. It can be used for hunting or in battle. A simple bow is a strip of material that will bend, such as wood, with a piece of string tied tightly to each end. It shoots an arrow, which is a piece of wood with a sharp point. Some scientists think that the bow and arrow dates back to 25,000 BC. Others think it was invented later, perhaps by the Egyptians around 5000 BC.
Modern bows and arrows are made from materials such as fibreglass and aluminium.

braces *noun*
1. Braces are strips of cloth or leather, that are worn with a pair of trousers. The braces are hooked over the shoulders of the wearer, and hold the trousers up.
Braces first appeared around the year 1726.
2. Braces are short pieces of wire and plastic that are worn around teeth. Over time, tightening the brace straightens the teeth.
He wore braces on his teeth to make them grow straight.

braille *noun*
Braille is an **alphabet** that can be read by blind people. It is made from patterns of raised dots. It can be used for writing words, numbers and music. Blind people read braille by touching the dots with their fingertips. Braille was invented by the Frenchman **Louis Braille** in 1824, and was published in 1829.
Computers can now be used to produce books in braille.

Braille, Louis (1809–1852)
Louis Braille was born in Coupvray in France. At the age of three, he was blinded in an accident. At the age of 10, he became a pupil at the National Institute for the Blind in Paris. While at the Institute, Louis Braille tried to find a way for the blind to read **books** by touch. He met an army officer, Charles Barbier, who described a way of sending orders at night by punching dots on cardboard. Louis Braille used this idea to invent **braille**, a raised alphabet, in 1824.
Louis Braille invented his alphabet at 16.

Bramah, Joseph (1748–1814)
Joseph Bramah was a British inventor. He was born in Yorkshire, and worked as a carpenter and furniture-maker. Later, he moved to London, where he owned a lock shop. Joseph Bramah's many inventions included a hydraulic press and a **banknote numbering machine**. He also invented a lock in 1784 that could not be broken into.
After 67 years, an American finally managed to pick Joseph Bramah's lock.

Braun, Wernher von (1912–1977)
Wernher Magnus Maximilian von Braun was born in Germany. In 1932, he started to work for the **rocket** programme at Peenemunde. This included the V2 rocket, used during the Second World War. In 1945, von Braun went to the United States of America to work on rockets.
Wernher von Braun designed many important space rockets, including Jupiter.

broadcasting   *noun*

Broadcasting is the sending out, or transmission, of **radio** and **television** signals. The history of broadcasting began with the invention of radio, in 1895, by **Guglielmo Marconi**. Television was first demonstrated by **John Logie Baird** in 1926. Clear, colour television signals can now be broadcast from one country to another across oceans by means of **satellites**. *Broadcasting is carried out from radio and television stations all over the world.*

Radio

In 1895, the Italian inventor Guglielmo Marconi sent radio waves over a distance of more than a mile. In 1901, he made the first radio transmission across the Atlantic, using Morse code. His transmitter was an electric spark generator.

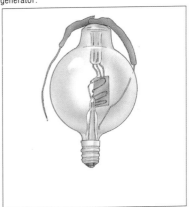

Broadcasting began in the early 1920s. Early 'crystal' radio sets had to be used with earphones for the sound to be heard clearly enough.

A radio of the 1930s was powered by large batteries. It was big and heavy.

By the early 1940s, families were gathering round a more streamlined radio set.

In 1954, a small device called a transistor replaced the large triode valve and pocket-sized radios could be made.

Television

John Logie Baird made the first television set in 1926. It was built of old cans, lenses, bicycle parts, string and sealing wax.

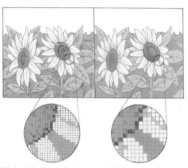

High-definition television, or HDTV, systems were developed in the 1980s. They give a razor-sharp image without any flickering, and stereo sound.

Very early television sets of the late 1940s had a small screen and large parts.

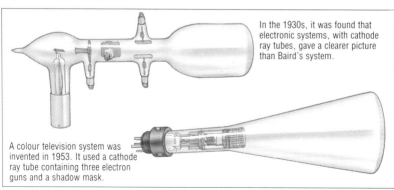

In the 1930s, it was found that electronic systems, with cathode ray tubes, gave a clearer picture than Baird's system.

A colour television system was invented in 1953. It used a cathode ray tube containing three electron guns and a shadow mask.

building techniques *noun*

Building techniques are the methods of making, or constructing, buildings, such as houses, temples, churches and offices. The first houses were probably built in about 10,000 BC. They were made of mud, packed into a wooden frame.

Building techniques have become so advanced that skyscrapers hundreds of feet tall can now be constructed.

Stonehenge, built in England between about 2800 and 1500 BC, was the first stone construction, using the stone-and-lintel method. By about 2000 BC, the Egyptians were building mostly in stone. They mainly used the pillar-and-lintel technique, but also knew about arches.

The earliest dwellings date from about 50,000 BC. They were tents made from a wooden frame covered with animal skins.

By 10,000 BC, sun-dried bricks, or adobe, were being used to build houses.

By 450 BC, the Greeks were using wooden beams in their temples.

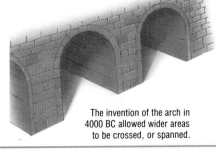

The invention of the arch in 4000 BC allowed wider areas to be crossed, or spanned.

In about 50 BC, the Romans were able to let more light into their buildings with groined vaults.

In AD 120–124, the Pantheon in Rome was one of the first structures to be built with a dome.

By AD 1162, huge cathedrals such as Notre Dame in Paris, France, could be built. This was the first use of the flying buttress, which allowed much higher walls to be constructed.

The Home Insurance Building, Chicago, USA, was the first skyscraper. Built in 1884, it had a 52-metre high, steel frame and rose to 10 storeys.

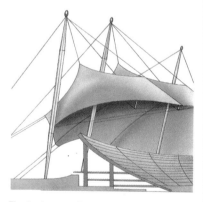

The development of computer programs has helped with the design of ultra-modern tension structures, such as the Olympic stadium in Munich, Germany.

brick *noun*

A brick is a small block that is used in building. Bricks have a rectangular shape. They can be made of mud and straw and dried in the heat of the Sun. Bricks can also be baked, or fired, in ovens known as kilns. Sun-dried bricks dating from about 7000 BC have been found at Jericho in the Middle East. Kiln-fired bricks were a **Mesopotamian invention**, of around 3000 BC.

Bricks are used for building all over the world.

bridge *noun*

A bridge is a structure that allows people or vehicles to pass over a river, road or railway. Very early bridges were probably made from tree trunks and strong creepers. The first bridge known to scientists was built in the city of Babylon in Mesopotamia around 2200 BC. It was built in the form of an arch.

Modern bridges include suspension bridges and cable-stayed bridges.

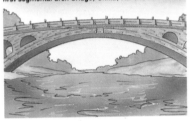

first segmental arch bridge, China, AD 610

broad cloth *noun*

Broad cloth describes fabric that is more than 140 centimetres wide. This is the distance that one weaver can pass a container of yarn, or shuttle, from side to side across a **loom**. In 1733, the Englishman John Kay invented a mechanized shuttle, or flying shuttle, which meant broad cloth could be woven much more easily.

Broad cloth is used for making clothes.

broadcasting ► page 22

Brunel, Isambard Kingdom
(1806–1859)

Isambard Kingdom Brunel was born in England. He studied in France, and then joined the engineering business set up by his father. Brunel designed **bridges** and built over 1,500 kilometres of **railway** track. He also designed three **ships**, each of them the largest and most advanced of their kind in the world. These were the 'Great Western', the 'Great Britain' and the 'Great Eastern'.

The 'Great Britain' was Isambard Kingdom Brunel's most important ship.

building techniques ► page 24

bulldozer *noun*

A bulldozer is a **machine** for moving earth. It is a **tractor** with a large steel blade at the front. Bulldozers can be used to push earth, or to drag earth backwards to flatten it. They can have **wheels** or caterpillar tracks.

Bulldozers were invented in 1923, by the American La Plante Choate Company.

bumper *noun*

A bumper is a bar of metal, rubber or plastic fitted to the front and back of a **motor car**. The bumper is designed to lessen damage if the car hits a hard object, such as another vehicle. Bumpers filled with air were invented by the Englishman Frederick R. Simms, and were fitted to a car in 1905.

Today, some cars have bumpers that are built as part of the bodywork.

Bunsen, Robert (1811–1899)
Robert Wilhelm Bunsen was born in
Germany. He studied science, and was
Professor of Chemistry at Heidelberg
University from 1852 until 1889. Robert
Bunsen was interested in gases and how
they work. He invented several kinds of
battery, and other scientific apparatus for
doing experiments on gas. The **bunsen
burner** is the most famous invention of
Robert Bunsen.
Robert Bunsen was a very good teacher.

bunsen burner   *noun*
The bunsen burner is a small gas heater
used in scientific laboratories. It is a metal
tube on a stand. A rubber pipe at the bottom
of the burner can be attached to a supply of
gas. A hole in the side of the tube can be
made larger or smaller by turning a metal
collar. Air is pulled into the tube when the
hole is open. The air mixes with the gas, and
burns at the top of the tube. The bunsen
burner was invented by the German **Robert
Bunsen** in 1855.
*The flame of a bunsen burner can be as hot
as 1,500 degrees Celsius.*

bus   *noun*
A bus is a kind of **vehicle**. It is designed to
carry many people along roads. Passengers
pay a sum of money, or fare, to travel on a
bus. The first buses were pulled by horses
and had eight seats. These buses ran in
Paris from the year 1662. A bus powered by
steam was built by the Englishman Walter
Hancock in 1831. Today, most buses have
an **internal combustion engine**.
*The Frenchmen Blaise Pascal and the Duc
de Roannez had the idea for the first buses.*

calculating machine ► page 28

calculator ► **electronic calculator**

calendar   *noun*
A calendar is a way of measuring time.
It divides time into days, weeks, months and
years. Most calendars are based on the
length of time it takes the Earth to ground, or
orbit, the Sun. The oldest calendar known
was an **Egyptian invention**. Some scientists
think it was devised as early as 4241 BC.
This calendar divided the year into 365 days.
The calendar most often used today is the
Gregorian calendar, invented by Pope
Gregory in 1582. Chinese, Islamic and
Jewish calenders are also used in different
parts of the world.
*The Gregorian calendar starts a new year on
1st January.*

calliper   *noun*
A calliper is an instrument used for
measuring. A calliper has two legs, held
together at one end by a rivet or screw. The
legs are often curved. They can be fitted
inside or outside an object. When the calliper
is taken away, the distance between the legs
can be measured. A calliper with curved legs
is used to measure the outside of an object,
such as a pipe. A calliper with straight legs
can measure inside an object.
*He measured the inside diameter of the pipe
with straight callipers.*

Calotype ► **photography**

camcorder ► **video camera**

calculating *noun*

Calculating is the working out of sums by adding, subtracting, multiplying or dividing. It became especially important when the buying and selling of goods, or trade, began. About 5,000 years ago, the **Mesopotamians** calculated by using pebbles placed in furrows on the ground. This led to the development of the **abacus**.

The abacus was the first calculating machine and is still used in China and Japan.

calculate *verb*

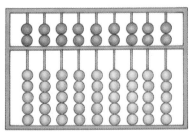

The abacus was probably invented in Mesopotamia as long ago as 3500 BC. The Chinese abacus was developed in about AD 200. It is a wooden frame with beads slotted onto rods. Calculations are made by moving the beads.

A calculating aid was invented in the early 1600s by John Napier. It was made up of a set of rods with the numbers 1 to 9 on the ends. Along the sides of each rod were the multiples of the number on the end. The device was nicknamed 'Napier's bones'.

In 1642, Blaise Pascal made a calculator to help his father. It had toothed wheels with numbers in rings around them. Numbers to be added or subtracted were dialled using the wheels. The answer showed behind holes above the wheels.

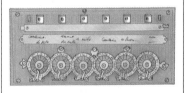

Today's electronic calculators can solve a wide range of mathematical problems. They are tiny computers, powered by batteries or solar energy and programmed with a silicon chip.

camera *noun*

A camera is a machine for taking **photographs**. Light passes through a hole or aperture, and through a **lens**, to fall on a piece of film that is sensitive to light. Large, heavy cameras were used by photographers such as **Daguerre** and **Fox Talbot** to take the first photographs. The first small camera that was easy to use was the Kodak, invented by **George Eastman** in 1888.
Modern cameras include polaroid cameras, cine-cameras and underwater cameras.

canal *noun*

A canal is a channel of water specially dug across land. Canals can be used for **irrigation** and for **water transport**. Locks allow boats on canals to travel up and down hills. The earliest canals were used for irrigation. The Nahrwan Canal between the Tigris and Euphrates rivers in Mesopotamia was built around 2400 BC.
The longest canal in the world is the Grand Canal in China, which is more than 1,600 kilometres in length.

candle *noun*

A candle is a source of light. It is made up from a fibre wick, surrounded by hard fat or wax. When a candle is lit, melted fat or wax is drawn up the wick to give a flame at the top of the candle. Some scientists think candles were an **Egyptian invention**.They have been in use since around the year 3500 BC. Most modern candles are made in moulds from paraffin wax.
Candle-making is a popular hobby.

candle clock *noun*

A candle clock is a method of **timekeeping**. A candle is marked in sections. Each section takes one hour to burn. A person can tell the time by looking to see how much of the candle has burned away. King Alfred of England invented a candle clock in AD 886.
For King Alfred's candle clock, six candles, burning at three inches per hour, were used each day.

canning *noun*

Canning is a way of keeping food fresh, or preserving it. Foods such as meat, fish, vegetables and fruit, are sealed into airtight containers made of metal. The containers are then heated to destroy bacteria or other harmful germs. Most cans used for canning are made of aluminium. Canning was invented by the Englishman Bryan Donkin. He used the bottling process invented by **Nicolas Appert** and adapted it for **tin cans**.
Bryan Donkin set up a canning factory in 1812.

cannon *noun*

A cannon is a large gun. The barrel of a cannon usually has a diameter, or calibre, of more than 2.5 centimetres. A cannon is placed on a carriage made of wood or metal. The carriage may have **wheels** so that the cannon can be moved about. Cannon were probably a **Chinese invention**. Cannon can also describe a heavy **machine gun** with a calibre of more than 20 millimetres.
Modern cannon are usually described as artillery.

canoe *noun*

A canoe is a small boat. It is light and narrow, and can be powered by paddles or sails. The dug-out canoe is made by hollowing out a tree trunk. It was one of the earliest forms of **water transport**. Canoes have been made from birch bark stitched to a wooden frame, and from skins covered with a waterproof substance such as fat.
Modern canoes are made from materials such as wood, or plastic strengthened with glass fibre.

an Eskimo canoe called a kayak, powered by a double-bladed paddle

car ► motor car

carbon paper
Carbon paper is a kind of **writing** material.
It is a thin sheet of paper, coated on one side
with substances such as powdered carbon
mixed with wax. Carbon paper is used to
make copies of letters and other written
material. It was invented by the Englishman
Ralph Wedgewood in 1806.
*Carbon paper can be used to make several
copies of a letter.*

carding machine   *noun*
A carding machine is a device that is used to
prepare materials for **spinning**. Fibres need
to be untangled and straightened before they
can be spun. Until the invention of the
carding machine, carding was done by hand.
Thistle or teasel heads were used, or small
boards covered with metal teeth. The
Englishman Daniel Bourne **patented** a
water-powered carding machine in 1748.
*Modern carding machines prepare both
artificial and natural fibres for spinning.*

carpet sweeper   *noun*
A carpet sweeper is a **machine** that sweeps
carpets. It is worked by hand. A carpet
sweeper is a brush placed in a box on
wheels. It can be pushed about by means of
a long handle. The brush sweeps dust and
rubbish into a container, which can be
emptied. The carpet sweeper was invented
in 1876 by the American Melville Bissell.
*Carpet sweepers are useful for cleaning
surface dirt on floors.*

carriage   *noun*
A carriage is a wheeled **vehicle**. Carriages
are usually pulled by horses, and carry
passengers. Before the 1700s, **carts** and
heavy coaches travelled on bad roads. When
better roads were built, smaller, lighter, faster
carriages could be developed. Some
carriages, such as the gig and the phaeton,
were developed for sport. Others, such as
the hackney carriage, could be hired.
*Carriages were an important form of
transport until the early 1900s.*

'square landau' carriage, 1780

cart   *noun*
A cart is a small, wheeled **vehicle**. It may
have two or four **wheels**, and is usually
pulled by a horse. A cart can carry a small
load. Larger loads are carried by **wagons**.
Carts were a **Mesopotamian invention**.
They first appeared around 3000 BC, in
Sumeria. Today the cart has been replaced
in Western countries by the motor van.
Carts are sometimes pulled by oxen.

cash register   *noun*
A cash register is a kind of **calculating
machine**. It has keys marked with different
amounts of **money**. When the keys are
pressed, the amounts of money on them are
recorded on a roll of paper, and a total sum
of money is calculated. A cash register is
used in shops to keep details of all the sales
that have been made. It was invented in
1879 by the American James J. Ritty.
*Modern cash registers are usually
electronic.*

cassette *noun*
A cassette is a small plastic box. It is designed to hold a long strip of **magnetic tape**, wound onto one reel. When the cassette is placed in a playing machine, such as a **tape recorder**, the tape unwinds onto a second, empty reel. Cassettes were invented by the Dutch company Phillips in 1964.
The word cassette can also be used to describe a container of film.

catamaran *noun*
A catamaran is a kind of **ship**. It has twin hulls, and can be powered by sails or by a motor. A catamaran can sail very fast. It was developed by the Polynesians. The design is based on the outrigger **canoe**. Some modern catamarans are a kind of **yacht**, and are used for sport.
A racing catamaran can travel at speeds up to 48 kilometres an hour.

catapult *noun*
1. A catapult is a forked stick of wood or metal. A piece of elastic is stretched between the prongs of the fork. It can hurl a small stone or other ammunition with great force.
Catapults can be used for hunting.
2. A catapult is a machine used in wartime. It could throw spears, stones or large weights. Some scientists think that the first catapult was a **Greek invention**.
A machine known as a catapult is used to launch aircraft from aircraft carriers.

CAT scanner *noun*
A CAT scanner is a **machine** for taking pictures of the inside of the body. It is made up of an **X-ray** machine, and a series of detectors. The detectors feed information about a patient into a **computer**. The computer uses this information to make a picture of sections through the body. The CAT scanner was invented by the Englishman Godfrey N. Hounsfield in 1972.
The full name of the CAT scanner is the computerized axial tomography scanner.

cathode ray tube *noun*
A cathode ray tube is a glass tube which contains a vacuum. When a strong electric current flows from the negative terminal inside the tube, a glowing light appears around the positive terminal. Improved cathode ray tubes are used in **television** sets and visual display units for **computers**.
The cathode ray tube was invented by the Englishman William Crookes in 1878.

cat's eyes *noun*
Cat's eyes are a safety device designed to help drivers to see the road. They are small pieces of shaped glass, or prisms, backed by mirrors that reflect light. Two pairs of cat's eyes, one to face in each direction, are placed in a domed rubber pad. This is sunk in the road, usually along the centre.
Percy Shaw invented cat's eyes after the shining eyes of a real cat saved him from driving over a cliff in a fog.

cat's whisker radio *noun*
A cat's whisker radio was an early kind of **radio** set. It could be made at home from materials that were easy to find. A piece of crystal was tied to a length of wire. The wire was wound round a cardboard tube. The cat's whisker was a piece of very fine wire. It joined the crystal on one end of the wire to the other end, passing through a pair of **headphones**.
The cat's whisker radio can also be called a crystal radio set.

Cayley, Sir George (1773–1857)

Sir George Cayley was born near Scarborough in England. He spent most of his life trying out ideas about **flight** and flying machines. He wrote about **helicopters** and **parachutes**. He designed a biplane, but had no means of giving it enough energy to fly. In 1853, Cayley made a large **glider** that carried his coachman 500 metres.
Sir George Cayley is often called the father of modern aeronautics.

Celsius, Anders (1701–1744)

Anders Celsius was a Swedish astronomer. In 1742, he invented the centigrade scale for measuring temperature. This is now known as the Celsius scale. Anders Celsius made 0 the boiling point of water, and 100 the freezing point of water on his scale. In 1743, Jean Pierre Christin turned these two round, to give the scale used today.
Anders Celsius is better known for his temperature scale than for his astronomy.

cement   *noun*

Cement is a soft paste of powdered minerals mixed with water. It is used to stick solid objects, such as **bricks**, together. When the cement paste dries, it sets hard and holds the objects firmly in place. When cement is mixed with sand and water, it forms mortar. Mortar was in use around 7000 BC, to build brick houses in Jericho.
Cements can be made that will set hard under water, or at very high temperatures.

central heating   *noun*

Central heating is a kind of **air conditioning**. In central heating, heat is carried through a building by water, steam or air. Fuels, such as coal, gas or straw, can be burned to heat water in a boiler. The hot water can be passed through a system of pipes and radiators, or circulated. The Romans invented a kind of central heating called a **hypocaust**.
In one type of central heating, hot air is circulated by fans.

ceramics   *plural noun*

Ceramics are a group of non-metallic chemicals that can be baked, or fired, at high temperatures. They include **brick**, **cement**, **glass** and **porcelain**. The earliest ceramics come from central Europe, and date from about 27,000 BC. The earliest use of clay to make fired pots was in about 7000 BC, in a part of Western Asia now called Kurdistan.
Ceramics, metals and plastics are the three most important engineering materials.

champagne   *noun*

Champagne is a kind of wine. It is usually a fizzy, or sparkling, wine, from the Champagne district of France. The bubbles in champagne are carbon dioxide gas. To make the bubbles, sugar and yeast are added to wine when it has been put into bottles or tanks. Champagne was invented by the Frenchman Dom Pierre Pérignon, a monk at the Benedictine Abbey of Hautvilliers, Champagne, in 1688.
Champagne is a popular drink at celebrations such as weddings.

chariot *noun*
A chariot is a wheeled **vehicle**. It may have two or four **wheels**, and it is usually pulled by a horse. Chariots were a **Mesopotamian invention**, first used around 2350 BC. They were used in warfare by many ancient peoples in the Middle East. Chariot racing became a popular sport, particularly in Ancient Rome.
Some war chariots had blades like knives attached to their wheels.

cheque *noun*
A cheque is a kind of bill of exchange. It is a written order to a **bank** from one person or organization, telling the bank to pay money to another person or organization. A cheque is usually a small piece of printed paper. A number of these are placed in a book. The first known cheque was written in London, in 1659. Nicholas Vanacher ordered his bank to pay £400 to Mr Delboe.
The first printed cheque was issued by Hoare's Bank in London in 1763.

chess *noun*
Chess is a board **game** that needs great skill. Sixteen white and sixteen coloured pieces are moved about a board of 64 light and dark squares. Each piece can only move in a particular way. The purpose of the game is to trap, or checkmate, the chief piece, or king, of the other player.
Chess is thought to have been invented in China, in the AD 600s.

chewing gum *noun*
Chewing gum is a soft, rubbery substance that some people enjoy chewing. Chewing gum is never swallowed. It is said to help people to concentrate and to relax. The Ancient Greeks chewed a gum they made from the sap, or resin, of the mastic tree. Modern chewing gum was invented by the American Thomas Adams in 1870. He made it from chicle, a gum that was chewed by the Maya Indians of Mexico before AD 900.
Today, chewing gum is usually flavoured with mint or fruit flavours.

Chinese invention *noun*
Chinese invention has given the world many important machines and substances. The four most important Chinese inventions are **gunpowder**, the **magnetic compass**, **paper**, and **printing** from **moveable type**. Other important inventions from China include the **horse collar**, **porcelain** and the **seismograph**. Many Chinese inventions spread westwards.
Chinese invention took place over more than 4,000 years.

Christmas card *noun*
A Christmas card is a kind of greeting. It is sent at the festival of Christmas, to friends and family. A Christmas card is usually a picture and a greeting printed on a piece of card. It was invented by the Englishman Sir Henry Cole in 1843. Today, Christmas cards are sent out all over the world.
The first Christmas card had a picture of a family eating a meal together.

Christmas cracker *noun*
A Christmas cracker is a paper tube, wrapped around a small toy. It also contains two pieces of paper that make a snapping noise when they are pulled apart. Christmas crackers were invented by the Englishman Tom Smith in the 1840s. Today, crackers usually contain a paper hat and a riddle or joke, as well as a toy and a snapper.
Several million boxes of Christmas crackers are sold each year at Christmas.

chronometer *noun*
A chronometer is a very accurate **watch** or **clock** used at sea. It is used to find **longitude**. The idea for a chronometer was first put forward in the 1500s. The first successful chronometer was not made until 1759, by the Englishman John Harrison.
Modern chronometers are powered by quartz crystals.

clepsydra ► water clock

clock *noun*
A clock is a **timekeeping** device. Mechanical clocks are powered by weights, such as **pendulums**, or by **springs**. The time is shown on a dial, or face. Mechanical clocks need to be wound up to keep them going. Electric clocks are powered by **batteries** or mains **electricity**.
The first mechanical clocks were built in the AD 700s by the Chinese Yi Xing and Liang Lingzan.

clothing *noun*
Clothing describes all the things a person might wear. It includes garments, footwear, ornaments and decorations. In very early times, animal skins may have been used to cover the body. By about 25,000 BC, **needles** had been invented and clothes could be sewn.
The earliest known woven cloth was made in Turkey in about 7000 BC.

Babylonian   1500s

1200s   1800s

Coca cola *noun*
Coca cola is a drink. It was invented first as a hangover cure to help people who had had too much alcohol to drink. When **soda water** was added to the syrup, the medicine turned into an enjoyable drink. Coca cola was invented by the American pharmacist Dr John Pemberton, in 1886. It is now drunk in more than 135 countries.
Coca cola is still made from Dr Pemberton's recipe, which is a carefully guarded secret.

- always delightful -
Thirst knows no season

Drink

Coca-Cola 5¢

Delicious and Refreshing

Cockerell, Sir Christopher (1910–)
Christopher Sydney Cockerell trained and worked as an engineer. In 1950, he bought a small shipyard near Lowestoft in Norfolk. Cockerell was interested in finding a way to reduce the energy needed to drive a boat through water. He decided that the answer to the problem was to float the hull of a boat on a cushion of air. In 1955, he **patented** the invention of a **hovercraft**. In 1959, the first full-sized hovercraft was launched.
Sir Christopher Cockerell developed many different kinds of hovercraft.

coin *noun*
A coin is a kind of **money**. Coins are small pieces of metal. They usually have a disc shape. A coin is stamped with a value. It can be exchanged for goods or services up to the value of the coin.
The first coins were made in about 650 BC, in Lydia, a country in what is now Turkey.

collar harness ▶ **harness**

colour television ▶ **television**

comb *noun*
A comb is a flat strip of a hard substance such as wood, bone or metal. Along one edge, the strip is divided into teeth. Combs are used for arranging and cleaning the hair. Combs can also be worn in the hair as a kind of decoration or **clothing**. Scientists do not know who invented the comb. They do know that they were common in Egypt around 2500 BC.
Today, combs are often made of plastic.

combination lock *noun*
A combination lock is a kind of **security** device. It is a very secure **lock**. A combination lock has a dial with a series of numbers around it. To open the lock, the dial must be moved forwards and backwards to point to the right numbers. This makes up the combination of the lock. The lock will not open unless the correct combination is used. The combination lock was invented by the Englishman **Joseph Bramah** in 1784. Some modern combination locks are worked by **electronics**.
Most floor and wall safes have combination locks.

combine harvester *noun*
A combine harvester is an **agricultural machine**. It can cut a crop and separate the grains from the stalks in one action. A successful combine harvester was invented by the American Hiram Moore in 1838. It was pulled by 20 horses. Today, combine harvesters are powered by **internal combustion engines**. They can cut crops in strips up to 5.5 metres wide, and harvest more than 12 hectares in a day.
Modern combine harvesters can cut crops such as beans and oil seeds, as well as grains.

communicating ▶ page 36

compact disc *noun*
A compact disc, or CD, is a disc on which signals can be **recorded**. The signals can be sounds, such as music. They can also be video picture signals, or information for **computers**. A compact disc is made of aluminium, covered with a layer of clear plastic. The signals are cut into the surface and are read by a **laser**.
The compact disc was invented by the Japanese company Sony, together with the Dutch company Phillips, in 1980.

compact disc player *noun*
A compact disc player is a **machine** that plays **compact discs**. It is usually a machine that plays compact discs that have been used to record music. A **laser** scans the surface of the disc, and the signals from the laser are turned into a **digital** electric signal. A portable compact disc player was made by the Japanese company Sony in 1984.
A portable compact disc player is small enough to carry in one hand.

compass *noun*
A compass is an instrument that can be used to find a direction. The simplest kind of compass is made of a needle that has been turned into a magnet. If the needle is placed in a bowl of water, it will point to the north. Later compasses had a needle placed on a card, marked with north, south, east and west, and points in between. The compass was a **Chinese invention** of about 1050 BC.
Modern compasses are built to stay steady even when an aircraft banks or dives.

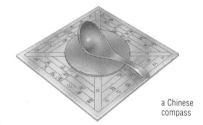

a Chinese compass

35

communicating *noun*

Communicating is the sending and receiving of messages. It is done by people when they speak to each other, person to person or down a **telephone** line. Communicating can also be done by machines, such as **computers** or **fax** machines. Messages can even be sent through space by **satellites**. Modern communicating began with the **electric telegraph** in the 1830s.
Smoke signals and beacons were early forms of communicating.

Samuel Morse (1791–1872)

In 1832, an American artist called Samuel Morse became interested in the idea of sending messages along electric wires. He made an electric telegraph, which used pulses of electric current to make a code of short and long dashes. This code was marked on a moving strip of paper on the receiving machine.

electric telegraph machine, 1840s

Morse code

A ●▬	J ●▬▬▬	S ●●●	1 ●▬▬▬▬
B ▬●●●	K ▬●▬	T ▬	2 ●●▬▬▬
C ▬●▬●	L ●▬●●	U ●●▬	3 ●●●▬▬
D ▬●●	M ▬▬	V ●●●▬	4 ●●●●▬
E ●	N ▬●	W ●▬▬	5 ●●●●●
F ●●▬●	O ▬▬▬	X ▬●●▬	6 ▬●●●●
G ▬▬●	P ●▬▬●	Y ▬●▬▬	7 ▬▬●●●
H ●●●●	Q ▬▬●▬	Z ▬▬●●	8 ▬▬▬●●
I ●●	R ●▬●		9 ▬▬▬▬●
			0 ▬▬▬▬▬

Alexander Graham Bell (1847-1922)

Alexander Graham Bell, an American speech teacher, was the first to make a successful machine to carry voice signals over electric wires. He patented his first telephone in 1876.

Bell's first effective telephone, 1876

1919 dial telephone

'300' model desk telephone, 1937

'trimline' push-button telephone of 1968

modern portable telephone

computer *noun*

A computer is a **machine** that stores and handles information. It also works as a **calculating machine**. Computers contain **silicon chips** that turn commands and information into numbers. Many people have had ideas for computers. **Hero of Alexandria** described a computer using **gears**. The German Konrad Zuse built the first working computer in Germany in 1941.

The first computer to be sold to the public was UNIVAC, built in America in 1952.

concrete *noun*

Concrete is a material used in building. It is a mixture of **cement**, water and crushed stones, or aggregate. Concrete sets hard when it is dry. It was invented by the Romans in about 200 BC. Today, different kinds of concrete can be made to suit special jobs. For example, reinforced concrete is used for building **bridges** and **skyscrapers**.

Reinforced concrete is strengthened by steel bars.

contact lens *noun*

A contact lens is an aid to seeing. It is a small **lens** made of plastic, that can be placed on the surface of the eye. The lens corrects faulty vision. Contact lenses can be used instead of **spectacles**. The Swiss Dr Eugen Frick made the first successful contact lenses in 1888.

It is usually very hard to tell if a person is wearing contact lenses.

cooker ► stove

corkscrew *noun*

A corkscrew is a **tool**. It is used for taking corks out of bottles. A corkscrew is a piece of wire, shaped like a **screw**. It has a handle at one end. The screw is twisted into the cork. The handle is pulled to bring the cork out. Corkscrews were in use by the year 1684.

Corkscrews came into use when corks were used instead of wax to seal bottles.

corrugated iron *noun*

Corrugated iron is a material used for building. It takes the form of thin sheets of steel which have been folded to give a wavy surface. The folds make the sheets stronger. Corrugated iron was invented by the Englishman Richard Walker in 1828. The folds were put in by hand, which took a long time. In 1844, John Spencer worked out a way of putting in the folds using rollers.

Corrugated iron is often used to make roofs.

cotton gin *noun*

A cotton gin is a **machine** designed to take cotton fibres out of cotton seeds. There are two kinds of cotton gin. In a roller gin, cotton fibres are gripped by rollers and pulled through a space that is too small to let seeds pass. A saw gin uses circular **saws** to carry the cotton fibres through a space too narrow for the seeds.

The cotton gin was invented by the American Eli Whitney in 1793.

crane *noun*

A crane is a **machine** that can lift and move heavy weights. It has a long arm attached to a heavy base. The arm can swing round in a circle. A hook at the end is attached to a **pulley**. Cranes worked by men walking in a treadmill were used by the Romans around the year AD 100. In 1845, the Englishman William George Armstrong invented a crane that was powered by water under pressure.

Cranes can be seen at most building sites.

crank *noun*
A crank is a part of a **machine**. It changes an up and down movement to a circular movement, or the other way round. A crank is a **wheel** that is attached by a pivot to a rod. As the wheel turns, the rod moves backwards and forwards. The crank is a **Chinese invention** from around 100 BC.
The earliest known use of the crank in Europe was around the year AD 830.

crash helmet *noun*
A crash helmet is a kind of **armour**. It is a helmet that protects the head of a person riding a vehicle such as a **motor cycle**. Crash helmets were first used during a race in France in 1904. Today, some crash helmets have shields, or visors, of clear plastic that protect the rider's eyes.
A crash helmet is well padded so that it is comfortable to wear.

modern

early 1900s

credit card *noun*
A credit card is a small plastic card that can be used to buy goods. It has a magnetic strip that contains information, such as the owner's name and address. A record is kept of the money spent and the owner must repay the amount over a period of time. Credit cards are an American invention. They were first given out in the 1920s by oil companies, so that motorists could buy petrol.
Banks and department stores can give credit cards to their customers.

crystal set ► cat's whisker radio

Cugnot, Nicolas-Joseph (1725–1804)
Nicolas-Joseph Cugnot was a French engineer. The French army was interested in finding a way to move **cannons** on land. The Minister of War encouraged Cugnot to make a **vehicle** powered by steam to do this. In 1769 and 1770, Cugnot made two vehicles, which were the first steam-powered vehicles to run on roads. The second of these **machines** was a gun carriage. It was a **tricycle** that could also carry four passengers, and moved at a walking pace.
Nicolas-Joseph Cugnot was a pioneer of steam-driven vehicles.

Daguerre, Louis (1789–1851)

Louis-Jacques-Mande Daguerre was a French painter and scientist. He became interested in **photography**. With Joseph Nicéphore Niepce, who had taken the first photograph ever made, Daguerre worked to try and improve the way photographs were taken. Niepce died in 1833, but Daguerre carried on the work.
In 1837, Louis Daguerre invented the daguerrotype photograph.

daguerrotype *noun*
A daguerrotype was an early kind of **photograph**. It was a sheet of copper, covered with a thin film of silver. When this was treated with the chemical iodine, the silver became sensitive to light. The sheet could be placed in a **camera**, and exposed to light for about 30 minutes. In this way, a photograph could be taken. Daguerrotypes were invented by the Frenchman **Louis Daguerre** in 1837.
One difficulty with making daguerrotypes was that no copies could be taken.

Daimler, Gottlieb Wilhelm
(1834–1900)
Gottlieb Wilhelm Daimler was born in Wurtemberg in Germany. He was interested in the use of petrol to drive **engines**. With Wilhelm Maybach, Daimler invented a light **internal combustion engine** in 1883. This was used to power the first **motor cycle** in 1885. In 1886, he made a four-wheeled car.
Gottlieb Daimler named the cars he made Mercedes, after the daughter of one of his customers.

damp-proofing *noun*
Damp-proofing is a way of protecting a building from damage by water. Builders place a thin layer of a waterproof material, such as slate, felt or plastic, into a wall just above ground level. Damp-proofing was a **Mesopotamian invention**.
Assyrian architects used bitumen for damp-proofing walls around the year 850 BC.

Davy, Sir Humphry (1778–1829)
Humphry Davy was born in Penzance in England. He studied chemistry, and from 1802 to 1813 he was Professor of Chemistry at the Royal Institution in London. Davy made many discoveries about chemicals and **electricity**. In 1812, Davy was asked to find a safe way of lighting coal mines. He invented the miner's safety lamp in 1815. Davy also invented the **arc light**.
Sir Humphry Davy's assistant was Michael Faraday, who became a famous scientist.

dentist's drill *noun*
A dentist's drill is a **tool** used by dentists. It removes patches of decay from teeth. When the decay has been drilled away, the hole can be filled with amalgam. In 1788, the American John Greenwood developed the first dentist's drill from his mother's **spinning wheel**. Modern dentist's drills are powered by compressed-air **turbines**. **Laser** drills are being developed.
In 1875, the American George Green invented an electric dentist's drill.

department store *noun*

A department store is a large **shop**. It sells many kinds of goods in different areas, or departments. Most department stores are in one building, which can be very large. The first department store was opened by the American Alexander Turney Stewart, in 1848. It was known as the Marble Dry Goods Palace, and was located in New York.

When Stewart opened his department store, it was the biggest shop in the world.

the Woolworth Building, New York, USA, 1913

derrick *noun*

A derrick is a kind of **crane**. It is a crane that stays in one place. The first derricks were used as cranes on **ships**. Later derricks were used largely for mining and boring holes in the ground. The modern derrick was invented by the American A.D. Bishop in 1850.

Oil derricks are used to raise and lower the machinery needed to drill an oil well.

detergent *noun*

Detergent is a cleaning substance. **Soap** is a detergent. Today, detergent usually describes an artificial cleaning substance that does not contain soap. The first detergent, which included soap, was invented by the German company Henkel et Cie in 1907. It was known as Persil. The first artificial detergent was made by the Belgian August Beychler in 1913. It was known as Nelcal.

The detergent Nelcal was invented when there was a shortage of soap during the Second World War.

dictionary *noun*

A dictionary is a type of **book**. It contains a list of words, usually arranged in the order of the **alphabet**. A dictionary explains what the words mean. It may give other details about the words, such as how they should be spoken. The dictionary was a **Chinese invention**. The first one was written by Pa-out-She, in about 1100 BC. It contained 40,000 entries.

The first European dictionaries were written by the Greeks.

Diesel, Rudolf (1858–1913)

Rudolf Christian Karl Diesel was a German engineer. He was interested in designing an **engine** that was more efficient than steam or gas engines. Rudolf Diesel invented a kind of **internal combusion engine** that was fuelled by oil. He took out a patent for this engine in 1892, and built a working engine in 1897.

Rudolf Diesel's engine is used for vehicles such as ships, locomotives and lorries.

difference engine *noun*

The difference engine was a **calculating machine**. It was designed to calculate and print mathematical tables without mistakes. The difference engine was invented by **Charles Babbage**. Although part of the machine was built, it was never finished. Work on it ended in 1832.

The difference engine was the first automatic calculator.

digital   *adjective*
Digital describes a way of using numbers to find answers to questions. All the information fed into a digital **computer** is changed into numbers, so that the computer can work. Digital systems can be used in devices such as **calculators**, and in some kinds of sound **recording**.
A digital watch shows the time with numbers.
digit   *noun*

diode   *noun*
A diode is an electronic device. It carries, or conducts, **electricity** in only one direction. A diode has two ends, or terminals. The first diodes were tubes containing a vacuum. Diodes today are usually made from **transistors** or **semiconductors**. The diode was invented by the Englishman John Ambrose Fleming in 1904.
Diodes are used in many machines, such as radios and television sets.

dishwasher   *noun*
A dishwasher is a **machine** that washes such items as dishes, cutlery and saucepans. Dirty objects are placed in baskets in the dishwasher, and **pumps** send strong jets of water and **detergent** onto them. The dishes are rinsed and dried once they are clean. The dishwasher was invented by the American Mrs W.A. Cockran in 1889. Today, some dishwashers contain **microprocessors** to control the heat and the flow of water.
The first dishwasher was made of wood.

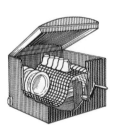

hand-operated dishwasher from the late 1800s

diving bell   *noun*
A diving bell is a **machine** that allows work to be carried out under water. It is a container shaped like a bell and open at the bottom. A pipe at the top of the diving bell allows a supply of air to be pumped into the bell from the surface. The first diving bell was described by the Greek inventor Aristotle in the 500s BC.
The first diving bell to be used was invented by the Italian Guglielmo de Lorena in 1531.

Sir Edmund Halley's design for a diving bell, 1717

diving suit   *noun*
A diving suit is a kind of **clothing**. It is a suit that protects a diver under water. A helmet covers the diver's head, and is joined to the suit. A pipe supplies air from the surface of the water. **Leonardo da Vinci** designed a diving suit in the 1500s. The first successful suit was invented by the English brothers John and Charles Dean in about 1820.
The modern diving suit is very similar to the Deans' design.

Dolby sound   *noun*
Dolby sound is a way of **recording** sound. Some **magnetic tapes** make a hissing sound when they are played. This is caused by grains on the surface of the tapes. Dolby sound stops the hissing noise on tapes. It was invented by Ray Dolby, an American living in England, in 1966.
A tape must have been first recorded using Dolby sound for the system to work when the tape is played back.

domestic appliance ▶ page 44

drain   *noun*
A drain is a way of taking water or other
liquids away from a place where they are not
wanted. A drain can be a ditch or channel
dug in the land to stop fields flooding or to
drain them. It can be an underground pipe
that carries waste liquid away from a building
or a street. Drainpipes are made of materials
such as fired clay, **concrete**, and **plastic**.
The Indus city of Mohenjo-Daro had a large
and well-designed system of drains around
the year 2500 BC.
Drains are sometimes surrounded by small
stones, to stop earth getting into the pipes
and clogging them up.

Drebbel, Cornelis (1572–1633)
Cornelis Drebbel was born in Alkmaar in
Holland. He worked first as an artist, then
became interested in science. Cornelis
Drebbel moved to England in 1604. He may
have brought the **microscope**, the
telescope and the **thermometer** to England.
His inventions include a machine for making
rain, lightning or thunder, and an **incubator**,
powered by steam. Cornelis Drebbel also
invented a **submarine**, powered by 12 men
with oars. It sailed up the River Thames
several times.
The submarine invented by Cornelis Drebbel
could carry 24 people.

dredger   *noun*
A dredger is a kind of **ship**. It is used to
make harbours deeper. It also keeps
harbours and estuaries free of mud. Most
dredgers have a chain of buckets that scoop
mud from the sea-bed or the bottom of a
river. When the buckets are full, they are
emptied into a barge beside the dredger.
A dredger was invented by the Flemish
Pieter Breughel in 1561. Today, some small
dredgers are hovercraft.
The first steam-powered dredger was
designed by the Englishman Richard
Trevithick in 1806.

Dunlop, John Boyd (1840–1921)
John Boyd Dunlop was born in Dreghorn in
Scotland. He trained as a vetinary surgeon,
and worked in Belfast, Northern Ireland. In
1887, he developed a rubber **tyre** filled with
air, called a **pneumatic tyre**. The first air-
filled tyres were made from pieces of
hosepipe. They were used on a **tricycle**
owned by John Boyd Dunlop's 10-year-old
son. Dunlop **patented** his invention. In 1889,
he began to make tricycles and **bicycles**
with pneumatic tyres.
The pneumatic tyre that was invented by
John Boyd Dunlop was soon used on motor
cars.

duplicating machine   *noun*
A duplicating machine is a kind of **printing**
machine. It makes copies of written or
printed material. To use a duplicating
machine, a master copy of the material to be
copied must be made. This is wrapped round
a drum. Paper is pressed against the master
and dye or ink makes a copy. The duplicator
was invented by the German company
Ormig Gessellschaft in 1923.
A duplicating machine can make about
5,000 copies from one master.

Dutch invention   *noun*
Dutch invention describes
the **machines** made for the
first time by the people who
live in Holland. Many Dutch
inventions date from the
1500s and 1600s. Dutch
inventions include drift nets,
the **microscope**, the
pendulum clock the
submarine, and the
telescope. The Dutch also
invented **windmills** for
sawing timber and the flat-
bottomed **yacht**.
The artificial kidney and the
artificial heart are important
Dutch inventions of the
1900s.

a pendulum
clock

domestic appliance *noun*

A domestic appliance is a tool or machine that is used in the home. Many domestic appliances have been invented to help in the preparation and cooking of food. Many others have been created to ease the labour of such tasks as washing clothes and keeping a house clean.

When electricity became widely available in the early 1900s, even more efficient domestic appliances could be designed.

Cleaning

The first electric vacuum cleaner was invented in 1901 by H. Cecil Booth. It was so large it had to be carried on a horse-drawn cart. An American called James Murray Spangler invented an electric vacuum cleaner small enough for home use. He patented his invention in 1908 and went into business with William Hoover.

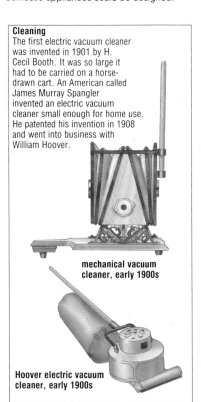

mechanical vacuum cleaner, early 1900s

Hoover electric vacuum cleaner, early 1900s

Washing and ironing

Electric irons were invented in about 1882. Electric washing machines were invented in the early 1900s.

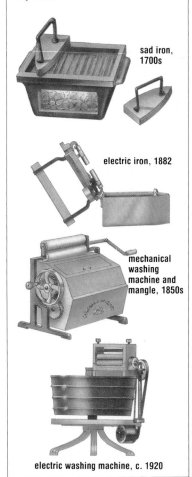

sad iron, 1700s

electric iron, 1882

mechanical washing machine and mangle, 1850s

electric washing machine, c. 1920

Cooking

Until the 1700s, people did all their cooking on an open fire. Then kitchen stoves were introduced. These burned wood or coal. In the 1880s, gas cookers were invented with a flame that could be controlled by turning a knob. The first electric cooker was designed around 1890.

solid fuel stove, 1700s

pressure cooker, late 1600s

electric kettle, 1921

halogenheat hob, 1980s

electric cooker, late 1800s

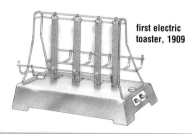

electric mixer, 1918

first electric toaster, 1909

tea-maker, 1904

dynamite *noun*
Dynamite is a substance that explodes. It is
used to blow up rock in mines and quarries,
so that miners can reach the valuable
minerals. Dynamite is also used to blow
holes in the ground for **canals**, dams and the
foundations of large buildings. Dynamite is
made from earths, such as kieselguhr, and
nitro-glycerine. It is usually shaped into
sticks, which are covered with wax paper.
Dynamite was invented by the Swede **Alfred
Nobel** in 1867.
*Dynamite is an important explosive in
industry.*

dynamo ▶ generator

Eastman, George (1854–1932)
George Eastman was born in Waterville, in
the United State of America. He became
interested in **photography**. In 1879, he
invented a machine that coated the glass
plates used in **cameras** to take pictures.
In 1888, George Eastman invented the first
small camera, the Kodak, that was very
cheap and easy to use.
*George Eastman made it possible for
ordinary people to enjoy photography.*

Edison, Thomas Alva (1847–1931)
Thomas Edison was born in Milan, in the
United States of America. He went to school
for only three months. At the age of 16, he
became a **telegraph** operator on the
railways. This taught him about **electricity**
and the telegraph. Edison's most important
inventions were the **phonograph** and the
electric **light bulb**. By the time he died,
Edison had taken out **patents** on 1,093
inventions.
*Thomas Alva Edison was one of the most
important inventors of all times.*

Egyptian invention *noun*
Egyptian invention describes a wide range of
tools and **machines** invented in Ancient
Egypt. Egypt was the place of one of the
world's first civilizations. It existed for over
2,000 years. The Ancient Egyptians invented
a **calendar**, and a way of **writing**, called
hieroglyphics. They found ways of building
large structures, such as **canals** and
pyramids.
*Many Egyptian inventions can be seen in
paintings on the walls of tombs.*

electric car   *noun*
An electric car is a **vehicle** powered by **electricity**. It became possible to build a practical electric car when a special kind of electric **battery** was invented in the 1880s. This battery could be recharged with electricity. The first electric car was built by the Englishman Sir David Salomons in 1874. Electric cars are cheaper and cleaner to run than petrol-driven cars.
At present, an electric car can travel about 120 kilometres before the battery runs out.

Detroit Electric car, USA, 1914

electric light   *noun*
Electric light is a kind of **lighting**. It is produced by using **electricity**. Most electric light comes from **light bulbs**. Some comes from **arc lights**, and some from fluorescent lights. Electric light bulbs were invented in America by **Thomas Alva Edison** and in England by **Joseph Swan**, both in the year 1879. Today, electric light from light-emitting **diodes** can be used to make letters and numbers on machines such as **computers**.
Electric light is cheap and clean.

electric motor   *noun*
An electric motor is a machine that works by **electricity**. It changes electrical energy into mechanical energy. Motors can be driven by electricity from **batteries** or from the mains supply. **Trains**, **trams** and many devices in the home are powered by electric motors. The first electric motor was built by the English scientist **Michael Faraday** in 1821.
An electric toothbrush is driven by a tiny electric motor.

electric telegraph   *noun*
An electric telegraph is a **machine** that sends messages by **electricity**. Messages are sent using signals in code, such as the **Morse code**. When the message is received, it is turned back to letters and numbers that can be read in the usual way. The first effective telegraph was invented by the American **Samuel Morse** and used in public in 1837.
Today, electric telegraph signals are sent on telephone lines, or by radio.

electricity ▶ page 48

electroencephalograph   *noun*
An electroencephalograph is a **machine** that records electrical activity from the brain. Small metal plates called electrodes are placed on a patient's scalp. They pick up electric signals. Pens scribble the pattern of the signals onto a sheet of paper. The electroencephalograph was invented by the German Professor Hans Berger in 1929.
Electroencephalographs are used by doctors to study changes in the brain.

electromagnet   *noun*
An electromagnet is a piece of metal that is turned into a magnet when an electric current is passed through it. Electromagnets are used in many **machines**, such as electric bells and **generators**. The electromagnet was invented by the Englishman William Sturgeon in 1825.
An electromagnet can lift many times its own weight.

electron microscope   *noun*
An electron microscope is an **optical invention**. It uses a beam of electrons to enlarge, or magnify, an object. The electron microscope can be used to view objects that are too small to be seen using light waves. It was invented by the Germans Max Knoll and Ernst Ruska in 1929.
An electron microscope allows scientists to see objects as small as bacteria and atoms.

47

electricity   *noun*

Electricity is a kind of energy. Most electricity takes the form of a flow of tiny particles, called electrons. Electricity can be made in generators. It can flow along wires in the form of an electric current. Electricity was first described by the Greeks around 500 BC. Since that time, many scientists have added to the world's knowledge of electricity. Today, electricity is used in homes, industry, transport, communications and science.
An English doctor, Sir Thomas Browne, invented the word 'electricity' in 1646.

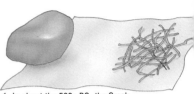

1. In about the 500s BC, the Greek Thales discovered static electricity. A piece of amber rubbed with cloth attracted small bits of straw.

9. By the 1960s, the tiny transistor was being used instead of the vacuum tube in nearly all radios and televisions.

10. Some microprocessors are so small they can fit through the eye of a darning needle. They combined several transistors on one tiny chip of silicon.

7. The development of the light bulb, or incandescent lamp, by Thomas Edison in 1879, led to the need for large-scale power stations to supply homes with electricity. The first was built in New York, USA, in 1882.

8. The invention of the vacuum tube in the early 1900s led to the development of radio and television.

2. A simple device called the Leyden jar was invented in 1746. It stored an electric charge.

3. In 1800, the Italian Alessandro Volta invented the first battery, known as the voltaic pile.

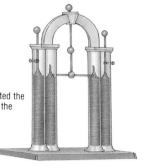

4. In 1821, the English scientist Michael Faraday invented the first electric motor.

6. In 1832, H. Pixii of France made the first practical dynamo for generating electricity.

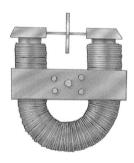

5. In 1823, W. Sturgeon made the first electromagnet.

electronic calculator   *noun*
An electronic calculator is a **calculating machine**. It uses tiny electronic circuits to add, subtract, multiply and divide. A calculator can also do more difficult kinds of arithmetic, such as working out percentages and finding square roots. The first electronic calculator was made in 1952 by the French Compagnie Bull. The first calculator put on sale to the public was made in England in 1961 by Sunlock Comptometer Ltd.
Each day, many people use calculators.

electronics   *noun*
Electronics describes a kind of science. It is the study of how tiny particles called electrons flow through different materials. The electrons can carry signals, such as sounds or pictures. Machines that use electronics include **televisions**, **computers** and **X-ray** apparatus. Electronic machines work quickly and accurately.
Electronics now forms a very large and fast-growing industry.

electroplating   *noun*
Electroplating is a way of coating one metal with a thin layer of another metal. Each metal is placed in a liquid called electrolyte. An electric current is passed through the liquid, and one metal becomes coated, or plated, with the other. Electroplating was invented by the Englishman John Wright in 1840.
The copper pot was given a silver surface by electroplating.

elevator   *noun*
An elevator, or lift, is a form of transport. It is a box or car that moves up and down in a shaft. An elevator can carry passengers or goods. Elevators are worked by **pulleys**, weights and **motors**, and powered by electricity. The first elevator was invented by the Greek **Archimedes** around the year 230 BC. It was not until the 1800s that elevators became common.
Today, elevators use microprocessors to work out which floors to stop at.

encyclopedia   *noun*
An encyclopedia is a **book**, or several books, containing information. Some encyclopedias cover all fields of knowledge. Others cover one subject, such as medicine or music. Some scientists think that the first encyclopedia was written by the Syrian scholar Abulfaraj in 1270 BC. The Greek Aristotle tried to put all existing knowledge into a series of books in the 300s BC.
Modern encyclopedias are written by teams of experts.

energy   *noun*
Energy is the ability to do work. There are several different kinds of energy, including light, heat, **electricity** and chemical energy. One kind of energy can be changed into another.
Electricity is a kind of energy that has often been used by inventors.

engine   *noun*
An engine is a **machine**. It uses parts that work together to change **energy** into movement. Some engines, such as those powered by steam, oil and hot air, are known as heat engines. They change heat energy into movement. Engines powered by petrol and oil are usually called **internal combustion engines**. The petrol or oil burns inside the engine. A hydraulic engine uses pressure from a liquid to drive machines.
Engines are sometimes called motors.

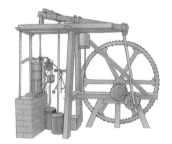

rotary steam engine designed by James Watt

50

engineer *noun*
An engineer is someone who uses science to make things that people can use. For many years, there were two kinds of engineer. Mechanical engineers studied and built machines. Civil engineers studied and built structures such as **roads** and **bridges**. Today, science has advanced so much that there are many more kinds of engineer. They include electrical, mining, chemical, biomedical and computer engineers.
They asked a computer engineer to mend their word processor.

eraser *noun*
An eraser is a small block that takes pencil, ink or chalk marks off substances such as paper. Rubber can be used to erase pencil marks. A powder made from volcanic lava, or pumice, can be used as an eraser for ink.
The rubber eraser was invented by the Englishman Mr Nairne in 1770.
erase *verb*

escalator *noun*
An escalator is a moving stairway. It is an endless belt of steps. An escalator moves people from one level to another. It can carry more passengers than an **elevator**, but it takes up more space. Escalators are usually found in public buildings, such as airports and stations. The escalator was invented by two Americans, George H. Wheeler and Jesse W. Reno. The first was built in 1894.
Modern escalators can carry up to 4,500 people an hour.

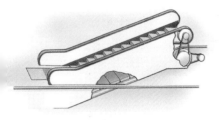

facsimile machine *noun*
A facsimile machine is a device that sends pictures and written material by **telephone**. It copies a document placed in it and sends electric signals to another machine. The receiving machine prints out a copy of the message. The facsimile machine was invented in 1843 by Alexander Bain.
A facsimile machine is usually called a fax.

fan *noun*
A fan is a cooling device. It makes the air move and causes a breeze. A fan that rotated was invented in China around the year AD 180. Fans of folded paper were invented in Japan in about AD 700. A fan worked by **electricity** was invented by the American Dr Schuyler Skaats Wheeler in 1882. This fan had two blades, and was designed to be placed on a desk. Now, most fans are powered by electricity.
People use fans to keep cool in hot weather.

Fahrenheit, Gabriel (1686–1736)
Gabriel Daniel Fahrenheit was born in Danzig in Germany. He studied in Holland, and lived in Amsterdam. Gabriel Fahrenheit was a physicist, interested in heat, light and other kinds of **energy**. He made scientific instruments for a living. In 1714, he invented a **thermometer** that used mercury to record temperatures. He also invented a scale for measuring temperature. This made 0 the point at which a mixture of ice, salt and water froze, and 32 the point at which water froze. The boiling point of water was 212.
The Fahrenheit temperature scale is named after Gabriel Fahrenheit.

false teeth *noun*

False teeth are artificial teeth that can be used in place of natural teeth. False teeth were invented by the Etruscans, a tribe that once lived in Italy, around 1000 BC. The German Philipp Pfaff described a way of modelling false teeth by making moulds in 1756. Modern false teeth are usually **plastic**.
President George Washington had a set of false teeth carved out of hippopotamus ivory.

Faraday, Michael (1791–1867)

Michael Faraday was born in Newington, England. He taught himself chemistry and physics while working as a book-binder. He became Professor of Chemistry at the Royal Institution in London in 1833. Michael Faraday made many discoveries about the way **electricity** and chemicals work together. Faraday's inventions included the **electric motor** and the electric **generator**.
Michael Faraday gave scientific lectures for children every Christmas.

fire alarm

A fire alarm is a device that signals a warning if fire breaks out. It can be a bell that makes a loud noise. A fire alarm can be a safety system that detects fire or smoke and sends a warning message to the fire brigade. An electric fire alarm was invented by William Channing and Moses Farmer in 1851.
In most countries, the law demands that places of business have fire alarms.

fire engine *noun*

A fire engine is a **machine** that is used to put out a fire. Fire engines usually carry **hosepipes**, **pumps**, ladders and tools, such as axes and **saws**. Ctesibius invented a fire engine around 250 BC. It had hand-operated pumps. A steam-powered fire engine, pulled by horses, was invented by the Englishman John Braithwaite and the Swede John Ericsson in 1829.
Most modern fire engines have diesel engines.

New York City's first fire engine, 1731

fire extinguisher *noun*

A fire extinguisher is a device that can put out a small fire. It is small enough to be held and worked by hand. Fire extinguishers spray water, foam or chemicals on the flames. The fire extinguisher was invented by the German M. Fuchs in 1734. He filled glass balls with water. These could be thrown into a fire.
Modern fire extinguishers were invented by the Englishman George Manby in 1816.

fire insurance *noun*

Fire insurance is a kind of protection. It protects against loss of money caused by a fire. The owner of a home or other building pays a small amount of money to an insurance company. If the building is damaged or destroyed in a fire, the owner is given an amount of money that may be as much as the value of the building.
Fire insurance was invented by the Englishman Nicholas Barbon in 1666.

firearm *noun*
A firearm is a light hand-weapon. It uses **gunpowder** to fire a projectile, such as a bullet. A firearm is made up of a barrel, chamber, breech mechanism and firing mechanism. Firearms include **pistols**, **revolvers** and **machine guns**. The firearm is a **Chinese invention**. The first gun known was made in 1288.
Modern firearms can use electricity and lasers to make them more accurate.

firework *noun*
A firework is a device that explodes to make a noise or a light. Fireworks are usually made from **gunpowder** and other chemicals packed into a cardboard tube. When the firework is lit, it sparks, cracks and makes coloured flames. Fireworks are a **Chinese invention**. The first fireworks were probably rockets, in use by 1150.
A Very pistol fires a kind of firework known as a flare to signal for help.

model Chinese rocket-launcher of the 1300s

flash bulb ► photoflash bulb

flight ► page 54

flight simulator *noun*
A flight simulator is a **machine**. It can copy all the stages of flying an **aircraft**. A flight simulator includes a cockpit with all the instruments a pilot may use when flying. It can also include engine noise, and moving pictures of what a pilot sees when taking off, flying, or landing an aircraft. Flight simulators are used to train pilots. The flight simulator was invented by the American Edwin Albert Link in 1929.
Flight simulators are cheaper and safer than aircraft for teaching flying.

floppy disk *noun*
A floppy disk is part of a **computer**. It is a magnetic disk inside a plastic envelope. A floppy disk can be put into or taken out of a computer. It can store information or commands for the computer. The floppy disk was invented by the American company IBM in 1970.
Floppy disks are widely used with personal computers and other small computers.

flying boat *noun*
A flying boat is a kind of **aeroplane**. It is designed to take off from and land on water. The body of the aeroplane supports it on the water. The first successful flying boat was the Flying Fish, invented by the American Glenn Curtis in 1912. Today, **seaplanes** are used instead of flying boats when an aircraft has to land on water.
Flying boats were used in many places where there were no runways or airports.

fork *noun*
A fork is a small **tool**. It is usually made of a hard material, such as wood or metal. It has a handle with a head at the top divided into two or more prongs, or tines. A fork is useful for holding down or lifting a substance such as food. Forks were used for cooking in the ancient world. The table fork used for eating was invented by the Greeks in Byzantium in the 900s BC. The Romans also used table forks. It was not until the 1700s that using forks for eating became common.
A large kind of fork with a wooden handle is used for gardening.

fountain pen *noun*
A fountain pen is a **tool** used for **writing**. It has a small tank, or reservoir, of ink. A narrow tube takes ink from the reservoir to the nib, so that the pen can be used to write. The first successful fountain pen was invented by the American Lewis Edson Waterman in 1884.
Fountain pens use thin ink that flows easily onto the paper.

flight *noun*

Flight describes the action of moving through the air. Powered flight includes flying by aeroplanes, air ships, and helicopters. It also includes flying using some spacecraft. In the earliest powered flight, people tried to use arms like the wings of a bird. Leonardo da Vinci designed a flying machine in 1492. The Chinese scientist Wu Han invented a flying machine in 1500. It exploded when it was tested. Today, rockets can fly into space.
Inventing ways of making powered flight has interested many scientists and engineers.

1783 — On June 4th, Josep and Etienne Montgolfier launched the first hot-air balloon. Made of paper, it ro 1,860 metres into the air. Later that year, they sent up their first animal and hum passengers in a balloon.

1969 — Concorde of the UK and France was the first supersonic airliner. It can cross the Atlantic in just over three hours, flying at a speed of about 2,000 kph.

Wilbur Wright   **Orville Wright**

1961 — The Hawker-Siddeley P1127 of Great Britain was the first Vertical Take-Off and Landing aeroplane.

1852 — Henri Giffard of France made the first flight in a steam-powered airship.

1891 — Otto Lilienthal of Germany made the first of a series of over 1,000 flights in a hang glider.

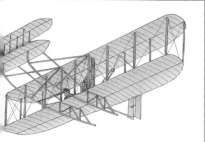

1903 — The Wright brothers, Orville and Wilbur, flew the first successful aeroplane. It was a biplane with a petrol engine. The first flight went 37 metres and lasted about 12 seconds.

1939 — The first practical single-rotor helicopter was designed by Igor Sikorsky of the USA.

1939 — The first successful flight of a jet aeroplane took place in Germany. It had one jet engine and was called the Heinkel He 178.

Franklin, Benjamin (1706–1790)

Benjamin Franklin was born in Boston in America when this country was a British colony. He had little schooling. At the age of 12, he started to work for his brother, a printer. Benjamin Franklin was a writer, publisher and politician. He was interested in education, and also in science. He studied **electricity**, and invented the lightning conductor. He also invented the **Franklin stove** and **bifocal lenses** for spectacles.
Benjamin Franklin was the 15th child in a family of 17 children.

Franklin stove   *noun*

The Franklin stove is a **heating** device. It is a box made of cast-iron that can fit into a fireplace to heat a room. Heat from the fire comes out through holes or vents at the back of the stove. Smoke goes up the chimney. The Franklin stove was invented by the American **Benjamin Franklin** in 1741.
The Franklin stove was designed to burn wood with little waste of fuel or heat.

freeze-drying   *verb*

Freeze-drying is a way of preserving food. It can also be used for medicines and drugs. In freeze-drying, the substance is first frozen, then dried in a vacuum chamber. Freeze-dried food looks and tastes better than food dried in the usual way. Freeze-drying was invented by Franklin Kidd in 1939.
Freeze-drying is expensive and not widely used.

frozen food   *noun*

Frozen food is food that has been preserved by freezing. Freezing food keeps more nutrients in the food than any other way of preservation. Freezing food using natural ice was a **Chinese invention** of the 700s BC. The British-born engineer James Harrison invented a **refrigeration** plant in Australia in 1850. Freezing food quickly was invented by **Clarence Birdseye** in 1924.
Frozen food has often been prepared so that it can be cooked at once.

fruit machine   *noun*

A fruit machine is a kind of slot machine for gambling. In a fruit machine, a player puts a coin into a hole called a slot. A handle is pulled that turns a number of reels. On the reels are pictures or symbols. When the reels stop spinning, a row of pictures or symbols shows at a window. If some of the pictures match, the player can win a cash prize.
The fruit machine was invented by the American Charles Fey in 1899.

Fulton, Robert (1765–1815)

Robert Fulton was born in Lancaster County, in the United States of America. He studied painting from the age of 17. In 1786, Fulton travelled to England, where he gave up painting and became interested in science and engineering. He invented **machines** for sawing marble, making rope and spinning flax. On his return to America, Fulton built a **steamboat** called the 'Clermont'.
Robert Fulton invented a steam warship, which was built after he died.

furnace   *noun*

A furnace is a device for making heat. Some furnaces, or **boilers**, are used to heat homes. Some furnaces are used to make products such as steel, glass and pottery. The earliest known furnaces were **blast furnaces**.
Furnaces can run on fuels such as wood, coal or gas, nuclear energy or solar energy.

Galileo Galilei (1564–1642)
Galileo was born in Pisa, Italy. He studied mathematics at the University of Pisa, and then became interested in physics. Galileo made better versions of the **telescope** and the **microscope**. They could then be used as scientific instruments. He invented a **thermometer**. Galileo made many important discoveries in mathematics and astronomy.
Galileo Galilei was put in prison for making his ideas and discoveries public.

game ► page 58

gas cooker ► stove

gas fire *noun*
A gas fire is a device used for **heating**. The mechanism of the **bunsen burner** is used to mix gas and air, which burns with a hot flame. Early gas fires were made up of strips of clay mixed with tufts of the mineral asbestos. These glowed in the flame and gave out heat. Today, gas fires can be made to look like burning coal.
A gas fire gives out heat as soon as it is lit.

gas lamp *noun*
A gas lamp is a type of **lighting**. It is a device that gives light by burning gas. Gas was first used to light a room by Frenchman Jean-Pierre Minkhelers in 1784. Gas lamps were made very much better when the German Carl Auer invented the gas mantle in 1885. The gas mantle is a tube of cotton cloth that has been treated with chemicals.
When a gas lamp is lit, the mantle glows, giving off a good light.

gas mask *noun*
A gas mask is a kind of **armour**. It protects the wearer from breathing harmful gases. A gas mask fits tightly over the face. Air can only enter through pads that clean and filter it, so the air is safe to breathe. A gas mask used to protect soldiers in the First World War was invented by the English company Robert Davis, Sieve Gorman in 1915.
Miners and fire-fighters often use gas masks to avoid breathing poisonous fumes.

gas street lighting *noun*
Gas street lighting is a way of **lighting** streets at night using gas. Street lighting makes it easier and safer for people to go about in the hours of darkness. It was invented by a German, Frederick Albert Winsor, in 1814. In 1812, he had set up the Gas Light and Coke Company in the United Kingdom.
London in England was the first city to have gas street lighting.

gas turbine *noun*
A gas turbine is a kind of **turbine**. A stream of hot gas pushes against blades set in a wheel shape. The **energy** of the turning blades can be used to power machinery, such as electric **generators**, **ships**, high-speed **motor cars**, and **jet aircraft**. The gas turbine was invented by the Englishman John Barber in 1971. Although he took out a **patent**, the turbine was never built.
Air is sucked into a gas turbine and burned with fuel such as oil to make hot gas.

game noun

A game is a pastime or amusement that people take part in, either by themselves or together. People have played games since ancient times. Board games, such as **chess**, have been played for hundreds of years. Playing cards were probably first used in China or Hindustan in about AD 800.
New games are being invented all the time.

In the 1500s BC, children in Ancient Egypt enjoyed playing a game of ninepins.

Billiard table games began hundreds of years ago, perhaps in the time of Louis XI. He was King of France in the 1400s.

Chess probably began in China in the AD 600s. But the game as it is today dates from the 1400s.

playing chess, from a French manuscript of the 1400s

fortune-telling tarot card, 1200s

jack of spades playing card, 1400s

Playing cards were probably invented in China or Hindustan in about AD 800. They spread to Europe in the 1200s, in the form of tarot cards. By the 1400s, cards like those of today were widely in use.

In the 500s BC, children in Ancient China were flying colourful kites.

A child in Ancient Greece played with this terracotta doll and horse in the 400s BC.

playing billiards in 1690

In Ancient Rome, children bowled hoops like this along the streets.

The game of mah-jongg has been played in China since about 500 BC. Small, rectangular tiles, engraved with Chinese drawings and symbols, are used like playing cards.

gear *noun*
A gear is a way of sending power from one
part of a machine to another. It is a **wheel**
or disc with teeth or grooves cut in the edge.
Gears work in pairs. The teeth of one gear
fit, or mesh, into the teeth of the other. When
one gear turns, it moves the second gear in
the opposite direction. Gears are known in
Greece around the year 100 BC.
Rack and pinion gears are used in the
steering mechanism of many cars.

gearbox *noun*
A gearbox describes a system of gears, or a
gear train. These gears can turn two rods or
shafts at different speeds. A gearbox is used
in machines such as **motor cars**. It allows
the motor car to travel at the right speed for
the road while the engine speed is high. The
word gearbox also describes the container in
which the gears are placed. The 1891
Packard motor car was one of the first to
have a gearbox.
The gearbox in the car had five speed
gears, plus reverse gear.

Geiger counter *noun*
A Geiger counter is an instrument used for
measuring. It measures radiation from
radioactive substances, such as uranium.
The Geiger counter was invented by the
German scientist Hans Geiger in 1912.
A better Geiger counter was made by
Hans Geiger and Walther Müller in 1925.
The Geiger counter can also be called the
Geiger-Müller counter.

generator *noun*
A generator is a machine that makes
electricity. An **engine** such as a **turbine**
turns a coil between the poles of an
electromagnet. As it turns, an electric
current flows through the coil. **Dynamos** and
alternators are two kinds of generator. The
dynamo was invented by **Michael Faraday**
in 1831.
Generators make almost all the electricity
used by people.

Gillette, King Camp (1855–1932)
King Camp Gillette was born in Fond du Lac,
in the United States of America. He worked
as a hardware salesman. King Camp Gillette
realized that only part of the blade of a
straight-edged **razor** was ever used. He
invented a razor with small blades that could
be thrown away after use.
In 1901, King Camp Gillette and his friend
William Nickerson patented the safety razor.

glass *noun*
Glass is a hard, clear substance made from
sand, soda and lime. These minerals are
heated until they melt together, or fuse, to
make glass. Many different kinds of glass
can be made. Flat glass is used for windows.
Fibreglass resists heat. Optical glass is used
for **lenses**. Glass was invented in Egypt and
Mesopotamia around 2500 BC. Today, more
than 100,000 kinds of glass can be made.
Glass is one of the most useful materials
ever invented.

glider *noun*
A glider is a kind of **aircraft**. It has fixed
wings and flies without using mechanical
power. It is kept in the air and moved along
by currents of hot air, called thermals. The
first manned **flight** was made in one of **Sir
George Cayley's** gliders in 1853. The flyer
had no control over the machine. The first
glider that could be controlled was invented
by the German **Otto Lilienthal** in 1891.
Gliders can travel hundreds of kilometres.

60

gnomon *noun*
A gnomon is part of a **sundial**. It is a rod or pillar. The shadow cast by the gnomon onto the marked surface of a sundial shows the time. Some scientists think that the sundial was an **Egyptian invention**. It was in use around the year 1500 BC.
The shadow cast by the gnomon showed that the time was 10 o'clock.

Goddard, Dr Robert (1882–1945)
Robert Hutchings Goddard was born in Worcester, in the United States of America. He studied physics at Clark University, and became interested in **rockets**. Robert Goddard made the first successful rocket powered with liquid fuel, which he launched in 1926. He went on to design larger rockets. His inventions include the first successful automatic steering device for rockets.
Robert Goddard believed that a rocket could fly to the Moon.

gramophone *noun*
A gramophone is a machine that reproduces sound. It uses a **needle** to pick up signals from a **gramophone record**. The signals are changed into sound and sent out by loudspeakers. The gramophone replaced the **phonograph** as a way of playing records. It was invented by the American **Emile Berliner** in 1887. Today, gramophones are being replaced with compact disc players.
Another name for a gramophone is a record player.

gramophone record *noun*
A gramophone record is a **recording** device. It is the flat disc played by a **gramophone**. The first gramophone records were made of a mixture of clay and **shellac**. Later gramophone records were made of **plastic**. A gramophone record has sound waves cut in it as a spiral groove. A needle placed in the groove picks up the signals. These are turned into sounds by the gramophone.
The gramophone record was invented by the American Emile Berliner in 1887.

Greek fire *noun*
Greek fire is a mixture of chemicals that burns fiercely when it touches water. It can burn under water. Scientists think that the first Greek fire may have been made of sulphur, resin, oil, pitch and quicklime. It was invented by the Syrian architect Kallinikos around AD 673.
The recipe for Greek fire was a secret.

Greek invention *noun*
Greek invention describes the ideas and machines that came from Ancient Greece. Ancient Greek civilization lasted from around 600 BC to about AD 500. Greek scientists worked out many laws of mathematics and physics. They made discoveries in astronomy and medicine. Greek inventions include the **aeolipyle**, the **Archimedean screw**, **cranes** and a **water clock**.
An important Greek invention was the great lighthouse at Alexandria in Egypt.

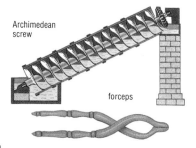

Archimedean screw

forceps

Guericke, Otto von (1602–1686)
Otto von Guericke was born in Magdeburg, Germany. He studied science, and was interested in air and how atmospheric pressure works. Otto von Guericke invented the **air pump**. He also showed how atmospheric pressure could drive a piston.
Otto von Guericke was the first person to make a vacuum successfully.

gun ▶ **firearm**

gunpowder *noun*
Gunpowder is a substance that explodes. When gunpowder is lit, or ignited, it burns very fast and makes hot gas. If the gas is in a small space, such as a **rifle barrel**, it cannot expand. This causes pressure which pushes out a missile, such as a bullet. Gunpowder was a **Chinese invention** of around AD 850.
Gunpowder is not often used today.

Gutenberg, Johannes (1400–1468)
Johannes Gutenberg was born in Mainz, Germany. There were many metalworkers in Mainz, and Johannes Gutenberg may have learned **metalworking** from his uncle. In the 1430s, he invented a mould for metal type. This could make many copies of one letter and letters could be arranged into words. Johannes Gutenberg also invented a **printing press**, like a wine press.
Printing in the way invented by Johannes Gutenberg spread quickly through Europe.

gyrocompass *noun*
A gyrocompass is a kind of **compass**. It is used in moving vehicles, such as **ships** and **aircraft**. A gyrocompass always points north, even when the vehicle moves in a different direction. It can do this because the compass has been placed on a **gyroscope**. The gyrocompass was invented by the German Hermann Anschutz-Kaempfen in 1908.
A gyrocompass is used to find a direction in a moving vehicle.

gyroscope *noun*
A gyroscope is a device that spins to keep a fixed direction. It is made up of a heavy **wheel** that has an **axle** running through it. The axle is joined to **gimbals**. These can move in any direction when the wheel is spun very fast. The wheel will keep on spinning in the same place. The gyroscope was invented by the German inventor G.C. Bohnenberger in 1810.
Gyroscopes are used to make gyrocompasses.

halogen lamp *noun*
A halogen lamp is a kind of electric **light bulb**. It contains a gas that is mixed with an element called a halogen. The halogen stops the bulb becoming black. Because they are small and give out a strong beam of light, halogen lamps are used for machines such as projectors and car headlamps. Halogen lamps were developed in the 1970s.
The bulb of a halogen lamp is made of a mineral called quartz, as glass would break in the heat.

hansom cab *noun*
A hansom cab was a kind of **carriage**. It could carry two passengers. The driver sat in a chair behind the body of the carriage. The hansom cab was designed to be very safe. It could not be overturned easily. The hansom cab was invented by the Englishman Joseph Aloysius Hansom in 1834.
Hansom cabs were often hired by people who wanted to travel about in cities.

Harington, Sir John (1561–1612)
Sir John Harington was a poet and an inventor. He lived at the court of Queen Elizabeth of England until 1584. In that year, he made the Queen angry, and she sent him to live in the country for five years. Here, he invented a **water closet** that could be cleaned by running water, or flushed. The water closet did not become popular, because few towns had a supply of running water.
Sir John Harington wrote a book in which he described his invention of the water closet.

harness *noun*
A harness is equipment that is put on a working animal, such as a horse. It allows the animal to pull vehicles and other machines, such as **carts** and **ploughs**. A harness is usually made of leather, held together with metal rings and buckles. It was a **Mesopotamian invention** of about 3000 BC. The earliest harness choked the animals, so they could not pull hard. The trace harness was the first reasonably efficient harness.
The trace harness was invented by the Chinese in about 350 BC.

harpoon *noun*
A harpoon is a weapon that is shaped like an arrow or a spear. It is used to hunt large sea animals. Harpoons were first used around 12,000 BC. Harpoons today are fired from guns. A modern harpoon was invented by the Norwegian Sven Foyn in 1863. It has a head that explodes when it hits its target.
The first harpoons were thrown by hand.

harpoon gun *noun*
A harpoon gun is a **machine** for firing **harpoons**. Most harpoon guns are powered by compressed air or by stretched rubber ropes. The first practical harpoon gun was invented by the Norwegian Sven Foyn in 1863.
A harpoon gun can throw a harpoon accurately up to 25 metres.

harvester ► reaper

hearing aid *noun*
A hearing aid is a device that makes sounds louder. It is used by deaf people. The first hearing aids were used in the 1600s. They were trumpet-shaped, and held in the hand. A hearing aid powered by **electricity** was invented by the American Miller Reese Hutchinson in 1901. A small hearing aid using **transistors** was invented by the American Sonotone Corporation in 1952.
Most modern hearing aids fit inside the ear.

heart-lung machine *noun*
A heart-lung machine is a device that does the work of the heart and lungs of a patient. It is most often used during surgery on the heart. A heart-lung machine takes the gas carbon dioxide out of the blood. It adds oxygen, and pumps the blood back into the body. The heart-lung machine was invented by the American Dr John H. Gibbon in 1953.
Open-heart surgery was made possible by the invention of the heart-lung machine.

heating ► page 65

helicopter *noun*
A helicopter is an **aircraft**. It is powered by spinning blades, or rotors. Helicopters can hover and do not need a runway to take off and land. A kind of helicopter was described in a Chinese book around AD 320.
Leonardo da Vinci drew a helicopter in 1483. The German Heinrich Focke invented a helicopter with twin rotors in 1936.
The first single-rotor helicopter to fly well was invented by Igor Ivan Sikorsky in 1939.

Vought–Sikorsky V5-300, 1941

Hero of Alexandria (1st century AD)
Hero of Alexandria was a Greek inventor and mathematician. He was interested in geometry and the scientific ideas used to make **machines** work. Hero's inventions include a simple **steam turbine**, a fountain, a water organ and a double-acting pump. He probably invented a screw press for squeezing juice from grapes and olives.
Several books by Hero of Alexandria still survive.

hieroglyphics *plural noun*
Hieroglyphics are a kind of **writing**. In hieroglyphics, pictures stand for, or represent, words and ideas. The earliest hieroglyphic writing was found in Egypt. It dates from about 3000 BC, but scientists know that hieroglyphics were used in Egypt for long before that date. Other kinds of hieroglyphics were invented and used by other ancient peoples, such as the Maya and Aztec peoples of Central America.
Egyptian hieroglyphics had 700 pictures.

holography *noun*
Holography is a kind of **photography**. In holography, a picture in three dimensions is made using a **laser beam**. The idea was invented by Hungarian-born Dennis Gabor in 1947. It could not be tried out because lasers had not been invented. The first holograms, or pictures using holography, were made by the Americans Emmel N. Leith and Juris Upatnieks in 1963.
Holography can be used to make three-dimensional pictures seen by microscopes.

Hooke, Robert (1635–1703)
Robert Hooke was born on the Isle of Wight in England. He was a scientist and inventor. Robert Hooke was interested in the way materials stretched, or their elasticity. He was the first person to see plant cells through a **microscope**. Hooke's inventions include an **air pump**, a **universal joint**, and an improved microscope.
Robert Hooke was interested in many kinds of science.

heating *noun*

Heating describes any method of making or keeping things or people warm. Wood fires were the first form of heating, used from prehistoric times when people first discovered fire. The Romans were the first to invent an under-floor **central heating** system, called a **hypocaust**. Coal replaced wood as the main fuel for fires in the 1800s. **Gas fires** were invented in 1853, electric fires in 1892.
Solar heating using energy from the Sun is the cleanest form of heating today.

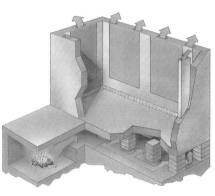

The hypocaust was the first central heating system invented by the Romans in about 100 BC. Hot air from a furnace flowed around a building inside a hollow floor.

In the 1400s, open wood fires were used for cooking and heating.

Oil was used for heating in this stove of 1890.

Radiators filled with hot water were a form of heating in the early 1900s.

The first efficient electric fire was invented by C. Belling of the UK in 1912.

Some houses today have solar panels on their roofs, which change the Sun's energy into heat.

horsebox *noun*
A horsebox is a container. It is a large box on **wheels** used to carry horses. A horsebox is used when it is not possible to ride a horse. It can be hooked on to the back of a vehicle and pulled along. The horsebox was invented by the English firm of coachbuilders Messrs Herring, in 1836.
The girl took her horse to the show in a horsebox.

horse collar *noun*
A horse collar is part of a **harness**. It is made of pieces of leather stitched together to make a U-shape. The collar is placed round the neck of a horse, above its shoulders. It allows the horse to pull much heavier loads. The horse collar was invented by the Chinese around 250 BC. It was first used in Europe around AD 1200.
A horse leans into a horse collar to pull a load with its shoulders.

horseshoe *noun*
A horseshoe is a U-shaped piece of iron that is fixed to the hoof of a horse. An iron horseshoe is heated and then nailed to the hoof. Horseshoes protect hooves and give a better grip on the ground. They were invented around 300 BC by tribes wandering in Asia and Europe. Nailed iron horseshoes were invented in Europe, around AD 500.
Today, some horseshoes are made of plastic and are glued to the hoof.

hosepipe *noun*
A hosepipe is a tube along which water or other liquid can flow. Farmers and growers use hosepipes for **irrigation**. Hosepipes are also used by fire-fighters to pour water onto fires. A hosepipe for fighting fires was invented by the Dutchmen Nicholas and Janvan der Jeijden in 1672.
A hosepipe made from gutta-percha was invented in 1850.

hospital *noun*
A hospital is a centre for supplying medical services. Doctors, nurses, and other workers care for sick and injured people in a hospital. The first hospitals were set up by Buddhists in India in the 300s BC. The oldest European hospital that is still on its original site is the Hotel Dieu in Paris, France. It opened in the AD 600s.
A hospital usually serves a community, such as a city, or a group of towns and villages.

hot-air balloon ► **balloon**

hot-air handdrier *noun*
A hot-air handdrier is a **machine**. It dries wet hands by blowing a current of warm air over them. **Electricity** is used to heat the air and to power the fan that moves the warm air onto the hands. The hot-air handdrier was invented by the German company Elektra Händetrockner GmbH in 1928.
Hot-air handdriers are a very hygienic way of drying hands.

hourglass *noun*
An hourglass is a device for measuring time. Two glass bulbs are joined by a narrow neck. One bulb is full of fine sand. The hourglass is turned, so that the sand is in the top bulb. It then takes exactly one hour for the sand to pour through the neck into the bottom bulb. The hourglass was invented in about 1306. It was first described by the Italian Francisco de Berberino in 1441.
Clocks and watches are now used instead of hourglasses.

hovercraft *noun*
A hovercraft is a **vehicle**. It floats on a cushion of air. A hovercraft can travel over land or water. **Turbines**, **fans** and **propellers** are used to make the air cushion and to drive the craft forwards. The English engineer John Thorneycroft thought of the idea for a hovercraft. He took out a **patent** in 1877. But he could not solve the problems involved in building it. The first, full-size hovercraft, the SR-N1, was invented by the Englishman **Sir Christopher Cockerell**, who launched it in 1959.
A hovercraft has a rubber skirt that holds the air cushion in place.

Huygens, Christiaan (1629–1659)
Christiaan Huygens was born in The Hague, in the Netherlands. He studied mathematics and law, and was interested in physics and astronomy. Christiaan Huygens invented a way of making better **lenses** for **telescopes**, an **engine** powered with **gunpowder** and the wave theory of light. His most important invention was the **pendulum**, to control the mechanism of a **clock**, and the balance-spring for **watches**.
Christiaan Huygens made many discoveries about light.

hydraulic accumulator *noun*
A hydraulic accumulator is a machine used in **hydraulics**. It gathers together, or accumulates, a quantity of hydraulic power. This allows hydraulic machines to work by themselves. They do not need a source of water.
The hydraulic accumulator was invented by the Englishman William Armstrong in 1850.

hydraulic crane *noun*
A hydraulic crane is a lifting device. It is a **crane** that uses water under very high pressure to raise and lower the arm, or jib. A hydraulic crane can move very heavy weights. It was invented by the Englishman William Armstrong in 1848.
Hydraulic cranes are often used in docks.

hydraulic engine *noun*
A hydraulic engine is a **machine**. It uses **hydraulics** to produce movement. Machines such as **elevators** and suction **pumps** use a reciprocating hydraulic engine. Another kind of hydraulic engine is a **turbine**, such as the turbine that works an electric **generator**. Early hydraulic engines used water to produce power. Today, hydraulic engines use fluids that do not freeze at low temperatures, such as oil and some gases.
The control system of an aircraft is a hydraulic engine.

hydraulics *noun*
Hydraulics describes a kind of science. It is the study of how liquids behave when they are moving and when they are at rest. In hydraulics, a liquid such as water is placed under very high pressure. It can be used to send, or transmit, power, from a **pump** to a **hydraulic engine**.
The engineer used hydraulics to design a water supply for the town.

hydroelectric power *noun*
Hydroelectric power is **electricity** that is made, or generated, by the **energy** of flowing water. Water from a source such as a dam is made to work a **turbine**, which drives a **generator**. Hydroelectric power was first used by the Frenchman Aristide Berges at his paper-making factory in 1867.
Hydroelectric power is produced today in the same way as it was when it was first used.
One-fifth of the world's electricity is produced by hydroelectric power.

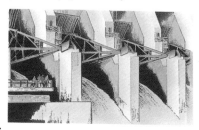

hydrofoil *noun*
A hydrofoil is a kind of **ship**. It travels with part of the hull above the water. A hydrofoil has wings, or foils, under the hull. As the ship increases its speed, the foils lift out of the water. The first successful hydrofoil was invented by the Italian Enrico Forlanini in 1906. A hydrofoil to carry passengers was designed by the German Hanns von Schertel in the 1930s.
A hydrofoil uses less engine power than an ordinary ship.

hydrogen balloon ► **balloon**

hydrometer *noun*
A hydrometer is a measuring instrument. It measures the density of a liquid. A hydrometer is usually a glass tube with a weight in the bottom and a scale on its side. It floats in the fluid to be measured. The density of the fluid can be found by measuring its surface level against the scale. The hydrometer is said to have been invented by the Greek woman scientist Hypatia of Alexandria in 460 BC.
Another type of hydrometer was invented by the Frenchman Antoine Baumé in 1768.

hygrometer *noun*
A hygrometer is a measuring instrument. It measures the amount of water vapour, or humidity, in the air. A hygrometer is also used to forecast the weather. It was invented by the Italian Francesco Folli in 1664.
One kind of hygrometer uses a human hair to measure humidity.

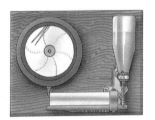

hypocaust *noun*
A hypocaust was a kind of **central heating**. Hot air from a **furnace** circulated in the hollow space under the floor of a building. Hollow tiles in the walls could be used to take hot air through the walls of a building, making it warmer. The hypocaust was a **Roman invention**.
Charcoal was burned in the furnace of a hypocaust.

hypodermic syringe *noun*
A hypodermic syringe is a **medical instrument**. It allows drugs to be given under the skin. A hypodermic syringe is a tube with a small piston or plunger inside, attached to a sharp, hollow needle. The hypodermic syringe was invented by the Irishman Francis Rynd in 1845. Modern hypodermic syringes are made of **plastic**. They are used once, then thrown away.
The doctor used a hypodermic syringe to give the boy a typhoid vaccination.

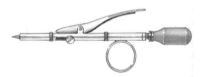

lever-action hypodermic syringe, 1800s

ice-cream *noun*
Ice-cream is a food. It is usually made of milk or cream, sugar and water, mixed together and frozen. Flavourings, such as chocolate or fruits, may be added. No one knows when ice-cream was first invented. The Italian traveller Marco Polo may have brought Chinese recipes back to Europe in 1295. Ice-cream was first made in a factory by the American Jacob Fussell in 1851.
She ate a large ice-cream flavoured with pineapple.

ice skates *noun*
Ice skates are a pair of metal blades that are fixed to the bottom of a pair of boots. Balancing on the blades, it is possible to travel quickly over ice. The earliest skates known to scientists were found in London, England, and date from around 50 BC. The blades were made of animal bones. Iron blades for ice skates were a **Dutch invention**. They were first used around 1250.
The first all-steel ice skates were invented by the American E.W. Gushnell in 1850.

iconoscope *noun*
An iconoscope was the first electronic **television camera**. It changed light images into electric signals that could be used to make a television image. The iconoscope was invented by the Russian-born American Vladimir Kosma Zworykin. He took out a **patent** in 1923. Today, better electronic television cameras are used.
The iconoscope was very important in the development of television.

immersion heater *noun*
An immersion heater is a **heating** device for water. A heater powered by **electricity** is fitted inside a water tank. When it is turned on, the heater warms the water. The electrical part of the heater is protected from the water by heavy layers of insulation. The immersion heater was invented in 1911.
Immersion heaters are used to heat small amounts of water in homes.

incubator *noun*
An incubator is a container. It is designed so that the temperature and the level of moisture in the air can be carefully controlled. Incubators are used in hospitals to protect babies who are born too early. Scientists can use incubators to grow bacteria in laboratories. The incubator was invented by **Cornelis Drebbel** in 1609.
Incubators can be used to hatch eggs.

Industrial Revolution *noun*
The Industrial Revolution describes a period of British history from about 1760 to 1830. During this time, people began to work in factories, and many power-driven **machines** were invented. Better ways of producing food allowed more people to work in the factories. **Mass production** of goods began. Good **roads** were built, and **canals** and **railways** were developed. **Banks** provided money to build new machines and factories, and an important financial industry developed.
Many machines and ways of working in use today date from the Industrial Revolution.

ink *noun*

Ink is a coloured liquid or paste used for **writing**, drawing or **printing**. **Pens** such as **biros** and **fountain pens** use ink. **Books** and **newspapers** are printed with ink, using **printing presses**. Ink was invented in Egypt and also in China, around 2500 BC. It was made from materials such as berries, soot and linseed oil. Today, there are thousands of inks, used for many different purposes.
Lithography uses an oily ink to print words and pictures.

invisible ink made of milk and lemon juice shows up when heated

ink cartridge *noun*

An ink cartridge is a small container of **ink**. It is made of thin, strong **plastic**. An ink cartridge can be used to fill a **fountain pen** with ink. The cartridge is placed in the pen, and is pierced at the top, so ink flows into the pen nib. The ink cartridge was invented by the Frenchman M. Perraud, of the Jiff-Waterman company, in 1935.
An ink cartridge is a clean and easy way to fill a fountain pen with ink.

instant coffee *noun*

Instant coffee is a drink. Hot water is added to powdered or **freeze-dried** coffee to make a drink of instant coffee. Powdered coffee is made by brewing coffee and driving off, or evaporating, the water. The crystals that are left are powdered coffee. Instant coffee was invented in 1938 by the Swiss company Nestlé, after eight years of research.
He put a spoonful of instant coffee into a mug and added boiling water to make himself a hot drink.

internal combustion engine *noun*

An internal combustion engine is a kind of **engine**. A mixture of fuel and air is burned inside the engine. This produces a hot gas that drives a piston or rotor. The piston or rotor turns a crankshaft. The first practical internal combustion engine was invented by the Belgian Jean-Joseph-Etienne Lenoir in 1860. A much better one was built by the German **Nikolaus Otto** in 1876.
Internal combustion engines can be fuelled with petrol or diesel oil.

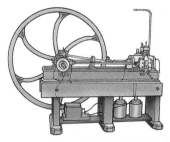

the Lenoir gas engine of 1860

invention *noun*

Invention describes the making of a new **machine**, process or product. An invention often uses known scientific laws, materials or devices in new ways. Many inventions have helped people to live more comfortably, or to do more and better work. The way people live today is the result of the many inventions that have been made throughout history.
Many important inventions were Chinese.
invent *verb*

inventor *noun*

An inventor is someone who makes an **invention**. Some inventors make one invention, which is given their name, such as the **braille** alphabet. Other inventors make many new things, such as **Leonardo da Vinci** or **Thomas Alva Edison**.
Today, inventors are usually teams of scientists working in laboratories.

iron *noun*

An iron is a device for smoothing out crumpled cloth. It has a smooth, heavy metal base, or shoe, which can be heated. On top is a handle, so the iron can be guided by the user. An electric 'Arc' iron was invented in France in 1880. This was very dangerous. A safe electric iron with a thermostat, a device that controlled the temperature, was invented by the Englishmen Morphy and Richards in 1936.

In the past, irons were heated in the fire.

iron lung *noun*

An iron lung is a kind of **respirator**, which is a machine to help people breathe. It is used when the muscles of the chest are paralysed, and the lungs cannot take in enough air. An iron lung is a metal tank. The patient is placed in the tank, and air is pumped in and out. The air pressure on the body allows the patient to breathe. The iron lung was invented by the Americans Phil Drinker and Louis A. Shaw in 1929. Today, smaller, electronic respirators are used.

The iron lung saved many lives.

iron plough ► **plough**

irrigation *noun*

Irrigation describes the way water is supplied to land so that farmers can grow crops. Some irrigation methods, such as the **Archimedean screw** and the **shadoof**, have been used for thousands of years. Today, trickle and sprinkler systems can be used for irrigation. These pump water along pipes and release it through small holes onto the fields.

Systems of canals and ditches can be used for irrigation.

irrigate *verb*

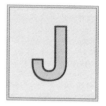

jack *noun*

A jack is a lifting device. In a screw jack, a handle turns a large **screw** fixed by a lever to a heavy weight, such as a car. As the handle turns, the force produced by the moving screw on the lever lifts the weight. A jack was first described by the Frenchman Villard de Honnecourt around 1250. Today, hydraulic jacks can be made that are powerful enough to lift houses.

She used a jack to lift the car so she could change the wheel.

Jacquard loom *noun*

A Jacquard loom is a weaving device. It allows patterns to be woven into fabric automatically. Needles, passing through holes punched in cards, carry a pattern onto the fabric. The Jacquard loom was invented by the Frenchman José-Marie Jacquard in 1801. He built a better loom in 1804. This loom has only recently been replaced with one controlled by **microprocessors**.

The patterns woven on Jacquard looms can be very detailed.

jet aircraft *noun*

A jet aircraft is an **aeroplane**. It is powered by **jet engines**. The first jet aircraft to fly was the Heinkel He178, built by the German Heinkel company in 1939. The first jet aircraft to take paying passengers was the de Haviland Comet, a British jet that came into service in 1952. Today, jet aircraft such as the supersonic Concorde can fly at speeds faster than sound.

The jumbo jet is a jet aircraft that can carry nearly 500 passengers.

jet engine   *noun*
A jet engine is a kind of **engine**. It sucks in air and pushes out a jet of hot gases. The gases are produced by a **gas turbine**. The first jet engines that could power a **jet aircraft** were invented separately by the Englishman Frank Whittle, and the German Hans von Ohain. Today, turbofans allow a smaller amount of fuel to be burned, while increasing the forward thrust of the engine.
A jet engine allows an aircraft to fly very fast.

jigsaw puzzle   *noun*
A jigsaw puzzle is a **game**. It is a picture printed on paper that has been glued onto cardboard or wood and cut into pieces. A jig saw is used to cut the pieces. The pieces have to be put back in the right order to make the picture. The first jigsaw puzzle was made to help children learn geography. It was invented in 1763 by the Englishman John Spilsbury, who cut up maps.
Jigsaw puzzles today can have thousands of pieces.

juke box   *noun*
A juke box is a kind of **gramophone**. It contains a large number of **records**, usually of popular music. A choice of music is made by pressing buttons on the juke box. A small charge is made to play the juke box. This is usually paid by putting coins in a slot in the machine. The juke box was invented by the American John C. Dunton in 1905.
He chose a song to play on the juke box.

jumbo jet   *noun*
A jumbo jet is a very large **jet aircraft**. It can carry up to 500 passengers or 91 tonnes of cargo. Some jumbo jets can fly for 8,700 kilometres before refuelling. The first jumbo jet was the Boeing 747. It was invented by the American Jo Sutherland and a team of designers in 1969.
Jumbo jets are named after a famous elephant called Jumbo.

Boeing 747 jumbo jet

kaleidoscope *noun*

A kaleidoscope is a toy. It is a tube in which coloured patterns can be seen. Two slanting **mirrors** inside the tube reflect coloured beads and pieces of glass held between two glass plates. The tube is held to the eye. As it is turned, new patterns are reflected in the mirrors. The kaleidoscope was invented by the Scot Dr David Brewster in 1816.
The boy looked through the peephole to see the patterns in the kaleidoscope.

kidney machine ▶ artificial kidney

kitchen range *noun*

A kitchen range is a kind of **stove**. It has a container for a fire, ovens, and hotplates on the top. Early kitchen ranges used coal and wood for fuel. The first enclosed kitchen range was invented by the Englishman Thomas Robinson in 1780. Today, kitchen ranges include the **Aga**.
Many people use gas or electric stoves instead of kitchen ranges.

kite *noun*

A kite is a kind of **aircraft**. It is made of material such as cloth or paper stretched over a frame. A kite uses the force of the wind to fly. It is guided from the ground by a long line. Kites have been used to carry measuring devices into the sky. **Benjamin Franklin** used a kite to prove that lightning was **electricity**. The kite is a **Chinese invention**. It may have been devised by Lu Pan, around 400 BC. Today, kite-flying is a popular sport.
Some Japanese kites are taller than people.

knitting machine *noun*

A knitting machine is a device that can make knitted garments. In a knitting machine, many more needles can be used than in hand knitting, and it can knit much faster. The knitting machine was invented by the Englishman William Lee in 1589. A circular knitting machine was invented by the Englishman Marc Isambard Brunel in 1816. Today, small knitting machines can be used at home.
A large, modern knitting machine can make up to 7 million stitches per minute.

Kolff, Willem (1911–)

Willem Kolff was born in Leiden in Holland. He studied medicine and became a doctor. In 1940, he began to work on a machine to clean the blood of a person with kidney disease. After five years, he had made a successful **artificial kidney**. At the end of the war, Willem Kolff presented six of his machines to different countries. He set up the first blood bank in Europe to help victims of air raids. He also helped to develop an **artificial heart**.
Willem Kolff emigrated to the United States of America in 1950.

Laënnec, René (1781–1826)
René Théophile Hyacinthe Laënnec was born in Quimper, France. He studied medicine, and worked as a doctor in hospitals in Paris. After seeing two children listening to the sounds made when they tapped a long stick, René Laënnec invented the **stethoscope** in 1816.
René Laënnec's first stethoscope was made of wood.

lamp *noun*
A lamp is a **lighting** device. It is one of the most important inventions ever made. Lamps can be fuelled with wax, animal fat or oil.
Gas lamps use burning gas to give light. An electric lamp gives light when **electricity** makes a filament of thin wire glow brightly. The first lamps were hollow stones filled with animal fat. They were in use around 70,000 BC. The **candle** was in use around 3500 BC. Today, most lamps are powered by electricity.
They turned on the lamps to give themselves light at night.

Landsat *noun*
Landsat is the name of a series of **satellites**. They give scientists information about the use of land. They also give details of where resources such as water and minerals may be found. Landsat satellites have sent many photographs back to Earth. Landsat was invented by a team of scientists working for the American space agency NASA. The first Landsat satellite was launched in 1972.
Landsat has been used to find good fishing areas and to map ocean currents.

laser *noun*
A laser is a device that uses light **energy** to perform tasks. It produces a thin beam of very powerful light. Lasers have many uses in industry and in medicine. They can be used to send television signals, cut metal and perform delicate surgical operations. The laser was invented by the American Theodore Maiman in 1960.
Laser stands for light amplification by stimulated emission of radiation.

the first laser, made in 1960

lathe *noun*
A lathe is a **tool**. It is used to shape materials such as wood and metal by turning them against a cutting edge. The lathe is a machine tool and may be powered by steam or electricity. Lathes were invented in the Middle East around 530 BC. Some scientists believe the lathe was invented by **Theodorus of Samos**. Today, lathes are worked by **microprocessors**.
A lathe was used to make parts for the refrigerators.

latitude *noun*
Latitude describes an imaginary grid of lines around the Earth, running parallel to the Equator. There are 90 degrees of latitude on each side of the Equator. Lines of latitude and **longitude** are used to find the distance of a point from the Equator. The first person to make a map with lines of latitude was the Greek Eudoxus of Cnidus around 350 BC.
The Equator is latitude 0 degrees.

launderette *noun*

A launderette is a place where people can hire a **washing machine** to do their laundry. The washing machines work when coins are put in a slot on the machine. The launderette was invented by the American J.F. Cantrell in 1934. Today, launderettes also have machines to dry clothes.
The student took a basket of dirty clothes to wash at the launderette.

lavatory paper *noun*

Lavatory paper is a soft kind of **paper**. It may be tissue paper. It is used by many people for drying themselves in a lavatory, or **water closet**. Lavatory paper was a **Chinese invention**. It was first described around AD 580. Modern lavatory paper was invented by the American Joseph Gayetty in 1857. Another American, Seth Wheeler, invented the lavatory paper roll in 1871.
Lavatory paper can be bought in several different colours.

lawn mower *noun*

A lawn mower is a **machine** that cuts grass. It cuts grass close to the ground, to make a lawn. The lawn mower was invented by the Englishman Edwin Budding in 1830. This had a revolving blade which cut through grass held against a fixed blade. Today, lawn mowers can be powered by **electricity** or petrol, or pushed by hand.
The Flymo lawn mower was invented by the Swede Karl Dahlman in 1963.

the first lawn mower

lens (plural **lenses**) *noun*

A lens is an **optical invention**. It is a piece of **glass**, or **plastic**, that has been ground so that one or both sides curve. Lenses can bend, or refract, rays of light to form images of objects. Lenses are used for many optical instruments, such as **spectacles**, **telescopes** and **cameras**. The earliest lenses may have been invented in Carthage in North Africa, in about 300 BC.
Plastic lenses were invented by the Englishman Arthur Kingston in 1936.

Leonardo da Vinci ► page 76

letter box *noun*

A letter box is a container. It is a box used for posting letters, **postcards** and small packages. At a stated time each day, the letters are collected from the box by a postman. Then they are taken to the post office to be sorted and delivered. Letter boxes were invented by the Frenchman François Vélayer in 1653.
She stuck a stamp on her letter before dropping it into the letter box.

lever *noun*

A lever is a simple **machine**. A rod or bar is placed on a support, called a fulcrum. If a force is applied at one end of the lever, a load or weight at the other end can be lifted. Levers include tools such as **scissors**. No one knows who invented the lever.
The Greek Archimedes worked out scientific laws about levers in about 240 BC.

Leonardo da Vinci (1452–1519)

Leonardo da Vinci was born near Florence in Italy. He studied painting and sculpture, and worked as an artist. He was interested in anatomy, architecture, engineering, mechanics, hydraulics, and many other sciences. In his notebooks are designs for many inventions, such as a helicopter, a parachute, a bicycle, furnaces, cannon, firearms with rifled barrels, machines for making coins, and a crane. The lock gates he invented are still used today.

Many people think Leonardo da Vinci was the greatest inventor of all time.

Wonderful flying machines

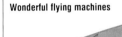

Leonardo had a lifelong interest in the flight of birds and a wish to make flying machines that could imitate bird flight.

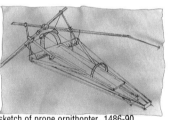

sketch of prone ornithopter, 1486-90

Parachutes

Many of the designs would not have worked if they had been made up. But two that did work as models were the parachute and the helicopter.

modern parachute

sketch of parachute, c. 1485

Fearsome war machines

First World War tank

Leonardo spent much time designing war machines and weapons. Some of these were so advanced that they would not have looked out of place in the 1800s or even 1900s.

sketch of armoured tank

American Civil War mortar

sketch of mortar

Tools, dredgers and diving gear

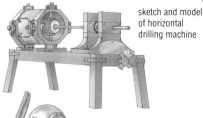

sketch and model of horizontal drilling machine

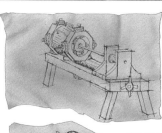

Leonardo designed a whole series of tools and devices using the elements of machines, such as screws, pulleys, gears, levers and ratchets. Many of these are similar to machines used today.

modern diving suit

sketch of diving suit

Leyden jar *noun*

A Leyden jar is a kind of **battery**. It is a device for storing an electric charge. A Leyden jar is a glass container sealed with a cork. Inside the jar are sheets of metal foil. An electric current flows down a brass wire running through the cork, and is stored in the metal foil. The Leyden jar was invented by the Dutchman Pieter van Musschenbroek in 1746, and by the German Ewald Georg von Kleist, also in 1746.

The Leyden jar is named after the city of Leiden in the Netherlands, where it was invented.

lie detector ► **polygraph**

life-jacket *noun*

A life-jacket is a safety device. A person wears a life-jacket to keep afloat in water and avoid drowning. Some life-jackets are filled with light materials, such as plastic foam or cork. Others are inflatable. They are filled with gases such as air or carbon dioxide when they are needed. A life-jacket has a shape like a vest or waistcoat, leaving the arms free. A life-jacket filled with corn was invented by the Englishman Dr J. Wilkinson in 1763. The first inflatable life-jacket was used by the British Royal Air Force in 1940.

She wore a life-jacket when she went sailing.

lift ► **elevator**

light bulb *noun*

A light bulb is a form of electric **lighting**. It is a glass bulb filled with a gas such as argon. In the light bulb is a thread, or filament, of tightly-coiled wire made of tungsten metal. When an electric current is passed through the filament, it becomes white hot and gives out light. The light bulb was invented by the Englishman **Joseph Wilson Swan** in 1878, and by the American **Thomas Alva Edison**, in the year 1879.

The filament in a light bulb may be coiled and then coiled again to give more light.

lighthouse *noun*

A lighthouse is a tower containing a light. The light guides **ships** at sea. Lighthouses have **lenses**, and reflectors such as **mirrors**, to strengthen the light of **lamps**. Lighthouses using open fires to signal were an **Egyptian invention**. The 122-metre Pharos at Alexandria, Egypt, was a **Greek invention** of about 280 BC. Today, most lighthouses are automatic.

Modern lighthouses may have radio or radar equipment to send out signals as well as a light beam.

a series of ramps led to the top of the Pharos

lighting ► page 80

lightning conductor *noun*

A lightning conductor is a metal rod. It is attached to a building to protect it from damage by lightning. A lightning conductor is fixed to the highest point of a building. It carries the **electricity** in lightning safely down into the earth. The lightning conductor was invented by the American **Benjamin Franklin** in 1752.

The power station was protected by several lightning conductors.

limelight *noun*

Limelight is a very bright form of light. It is made by burning a piece of limestone in a flame made from hydrogen and oxygen. Limelight was used in places where strong lights were needed, such as **lighthouses** and theatres. It was invented by the Englishman Thomas Drummond in 1826.

Limelight could be seen 180 kilometres away.

Lilienthal, Otto (1848–1896)
Otto Lilienthal was born in Anklam in
northern Germany. He studied engineering.
Lilienthal had been interested in the flight of
birds from boyhood. In 1886, with the help of
his brother Gustav, he built a **glider**. Otto
Lilienthal invented mechanisms that allowed
the glider flight to be controlled by the pilot.
He kept detailed notebooks that were very
useful to other engineers and inventors
interested in **aircraft**.
*Otto Lilienthal was killed in a gliding
accident.*

liner   *noun*
A liner is a large passenger **ship**. The first
liners were built during the 1800s. The
steam engine and the use of iron and steel
meant comfortable, fast ships could be
made. One of the first such liners was the
'Great Britain'. It was designed by **Isambard
Kingdom Brunel** and launched in 1843.
Liners cross oceans, working to set times.

Linotype ▶ **typesetting machine**

Lipperschey, Hans (1570–1619)
Hans Lipperschey was born in Wesel in
Germany. He worked as a spectacle-maker
in Holland. In 1608, Lipperschey invented
the **telescope**. The ruler of Holland tried to
keep this invention a secret because he could
see how useful a telescope would be to his
enemies. The secret could not be kept.
Hans Lipperschey also made a microscope.

lithography   *noun*
Lithography is a **printing** process. The
images to be printed are drawn on a printing
plate with a wax crayon. The plate is made
damp with water. Ink is rolled over the plate
and sticks only to the waxed part. The ink is
then transferred to paper.
*Lithography was invented by the German
Alois Senefelder in 1793.*

lock   *noun*
A lock is a **security** device. It stops an object
being opened or moved. There are many
kinds of lock. Most are opened with a key.
Locks were an **Egyptian invention**. The first
lock was made around 2000 BC.
*When she went out of the house, she turned
the key in the lock.*

lock ▶ **canal**

locomotive   *noun*
A locomotive is a machine that moves a
train. Locomotives have very strong
engines. They can be powered by steam,
electricity or diesel oil. The first steam
locomotive was invented by the Englishman
Richard Trevithick in 1804. The first
successful electric locomotive was built by
the German E.W. von Siemens in 1879.
*Robert Stephenson's steam locomotive,
'Rocket', had a top speed of 48 kph.*

longitude   *noun*
Longitude describes an imaginary grid of
lines around the Earth. Lines of longitude
start at the North Pole and finish at the South
Pole. Longitude is used to measure
distances eastward or westward. The first
person to mark a map with lines of longitude
was the Greek Eratosthenes of Cyrene,
around 240 BC. Today, longitude and the
vertical measurement **latitude** are used to
describe accurately any place on Earth.
*The Greenwich Meridian in England is
longitude 0 degrees.*

loom ▶ **spinning and weaving**

lighting *noun*

Lighting describes any way of bringing light to a dark area where there is no natural source of light. It allows people to carry on working and playing when darkness falls. In prehistoric times, people used fire for lighting the darkness. **Oil lamps** and **candles** gave a steadier light, but it was not bright enough to be of much use. **Gas lighting** gave a brighter, clearer light and was used from the 1780s.

The electric light bulb, invented in the late 1870s, revolutionized lighting.

The first form of lighting was a burning branch taken from a fire. People learnt to use bundles of reeds tied together and dipped in pitch or wax.

The invention of fluorescent lighting in the 1930s marked the beginning of the use of various gases instead of a wire filament inside a glass tube.

A modern electric light bulb uses a tungsten thread, or filament, which can burn more brightly. This was patented in 1913 by William Coolidge.

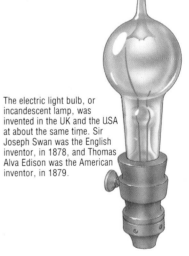

The electric light bulb, or incandescent lamp, was invented in the UK and the USA at about the same time. Sir Joseph Swan was the English inventor, in 1878, and Thomas Alva Edison was the American inventor, in 1879.

Oil lamps were made as long ago as 50,000 years, from a hollowed-out stone filled with fat. Pottery oil lamps were made in Iraq about 10,000 years ago. Wick oil lamps, such as this Roman one, were first made in about 1000 BC.

Candles have been used for lighting since about 3000 BC.

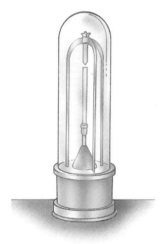

The electric arc lamp was invented by Humphry Davy in 1809. It was made up of two charcoal rods, each connected to one terminal of a powerful electric battery. The rods glowed white-hot when they touched. When they were drawn apart, an intensely bright arc streamed between their tips.

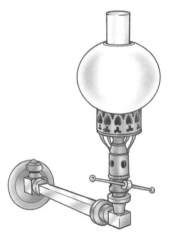

Gas lighting was invented in 1780 by a Scotsman, William Murdock.

McCormick, Cyrus Hall (1809–1884)

Cyrus Hall McCormick was born in Rockbridge County, in the United States of America. His most famous invention was a mechanical horse-drawn reaper for cutting grain crops. He built his first reaper in 1831. McCormick invented a number of other **agricultural machines**, including a hillside **plough**.

Cyrus Hall McCormick's reaper could cut as much corn as 16 people could using hand tools.

machine   *noun*

A machine is any device which performs useful work. Levers, pulleys, screws, inclined planes, wheels and axles are simple machines. More complicated machines are made by putting together, or combining, these simple machines. Machines which convert one form of energy, such as heat energy, into mechanical energy are called **engines**.

A drill is a machine for making round holes in wood, metal or other materials.

machine gun   *noun*

A machine gun is a small, rapid-firing gun. It fires cartridges one after the other.

Leonardo da Vinci made drawings of rapid-firing guns in his notebooks. The first entirely automatic machine gun was invented by an American-born British inventor Hiram Maxim, in 1883. Later machine guns were light enough to be fired while being carried.

The Maxim machine gun could fire up to 250 cartridges which were carried on a canvas belt.

magic lantern   *noun*

A magic lantern was an early kind of slide projector. It projected images from glass slides through a lens onto a screen. Magic lanterns were probably invented in the 1500s. In the 1700s and 1800s, magic lantern shows were a popular form of entertainment before the cinematograph was invented. The modern form of the magic lantern is the slide projector which uses film slides.

The magic lantern was often used to illustrate talks and lectures.

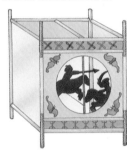

Chinese magic lantern, AD 100s

magnetic tape   *noun*

Magnetic tape is a long ribbon of plastic coated on one side with particles of magnetic material. Electric signals from a sound source, such as a microphone, change the position of the particles. When the tape is played through a **tape recorder**, the sounds are reproduced. Magnetic tape is stored on reels or in cassettes.

Magnetic tape was invented in Germany in 1935.

magnifying glass   *noun*

A magnifying glass is a **lens**. It makes objects look larger when it is placed close to them. The lens in a magnifying glass is convex. This means that it is thicker in the centre than at the sides. Magnifying glasses were used before **spectacles** were invented.

The pattern of a fingerprint can be clearly seen through a magnifying glass.

Marconi, Guglielmo (1874–1937)
Guglielmo Marconi was born in Bologna,
Italy. After many years of studying science,
he became the inventor of the **telegraph**. He
discovered that electromagnetic waves could
be used to carry signals. Marconi sent his
first signals in 1895. By 1901, he had sent
signals across the Atlantic.
*Guglielmo Marconi's system was used to
send messages in Morse code.*

margarine   *noun*
Margarine is an artificial food which is used
instead of butter. It is used as a spread on
bread, and in cooking. Margarine was
invented in 1862 by a French chemist,
Hippolyte Mège-Mouriés. He made it from
animal fat. Today, it is usually made from
vegetable oils.
*Margarine is sometimes mixed with a little
butter to make it taste better.*

marine chronometer   *noun*
A marine chronometer is a **clock** which
keeps time very accurately. It is used by
sailors to work out their position when at sea.
A marine chronometer must be able to stand
up to the motion of a ship and to changes
of temperature. The first successful
chronometer was made in 1759 by an
English clockmaker, John Harrison.
*John Harrison's marine chronometer was so
accurate that he won a prize from the British
Navy.*

English marine chronometer, 1777

maser   *noun*
A maser is a device for making a very
intense beam of microwaves. The word is
made up of the initial letters of the words
'microwave amplification by stimulated
emission of radiation'. The maser's sharp,
clear beam is produced by heating a gas to a
very high temperature. The first maser was
built in 1953 at Columbia University, United
States of America, by Dr Charles Townes.
*Masers can be used to strengthen weak
microwave signals from distant stars.*

mass production   *noun*
Mass production is the making of large
numbers of similar items, usually by
machine. Mass-produced goods take less
time to make, and so are less costly than
hand-made ones. The first manufacturer to
introduce mass production was Sir Marc
Isambard Brunel who set up a factory to
make pulley blocks for the British navy.
*The Ford Motor Company was the first to
make cars by mass production.*
mass-produce   *verb*

matches   *plural noun*
Matches are thin pieces of wood or
cardboard tipped with chemicals that burn
easily. The first matches, with phosphorus
tips, were made by a French chemist,
François Derosne, in 1816.
*Safety matches will light only if struck on
special material on the side of the box.*

medical invention   ► page 84

medical thermometer   *noun*
The medical or clinical thermometer is a
measuring device. It measures the
temperature of the human body. It is a
sealed glass tube containing mercury, which
is usually placed under the tongue. The
temperature is recorded on a **temperature
scale** printed on the side of the tube.
*The short medical thermometer used today
was invented in 1867 by a British doctor,
Thomas Allbutt.*

medical invention *noun*

Medical invention describes the tools, machines or other devices made for the diagnosis or treatment of sick people. The 1800s and 1900s have seen the greatest number of inventions in the field of medicine. Before the 1800s, doctors had few aids to help them in the fight against disease. Surgeons amputated limbs and pulled teeth with a few basic instruments, such as hooks, saws and forceps.
Medical inventions have saved many lives over the years.

1700s and 1800s

The first full set of false teeth was made in about 1780. The teeth were made of ivory and porcelain and so were very expensive.

Edward Jenner (1749–1823) discovered the smallpox vaccine that has saved thousands of lives. He began using it in 1796.

In 1819, the French doctor Théophile Laënnec invented the stethoscope for listening to a patient's heartbeat.

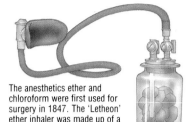

The anesthetics ether and chloroform were first used for surgery in 1847. The 'Letheon' ether inhaler was made up of a glass jar containing sponges soaked in ether.

Clinical thermometers for taking a patient's temperature were first used in 1863.

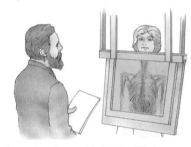

X-rays were discovered in 1895 by Wilhelm Röntgen, a German physicist.

In 1898, Marie and Pierre Curie discovered radium and radiotherapy began.

In 1903, W. Einthoven of Holland designed the first accurate electrocardiograph. This was a machine for measuring the heartbeat.

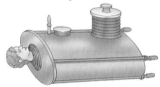

The iron lung was invented in 1929. It works the lungs of people who are unable to breathe on their own.

The first practical kidney machine was designed in 1943 by W. Kolff of Holland.

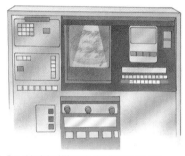

I. Donald of the UK made the first successful ultrasound machine in 1955. It uses high-frequency sound waves to make a picture of the inside of the body.

In 1957, the first pacemaker was placed inside a person's chest to control the heartbeat.

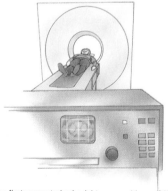

The first computerized axial tomographic, or CAT, scanner was developed in 1971 by G. Hounsfield of the UK. It is a machine for seeing inside a person's brain.

megaphone *noun*
A megaphone is a cone of material such as thin metal, plastic or cardboard. It makes the voice louder when a person speaks through the narrower end of the cone.
A megaphone stops sound waves from spreading out as soon as they leave the speaker's lips.

mercury vapour lamp *noun*
A mercury vapour lamp is a kind of **lighting**. It is a glass tube filled with a gas called mercury vapour. When an electric current passes through it, the gas gives off rays of invisible ultraviolet light. These rays strike a coating on the inside of the tube, which glows with visible light. Mercury vapour lamps are used for **street lighting** and also in medical treatment.
Mercury vapour lamps were developed in the 1930s.

Mesopotamian invention *noun*
Mesopotamian invention describes the ideas and tools that came from Mesopotamia. Mesopotamia lay in what is now called the Arabian Peninsula. It was one of the first centres of world civilization. The cities of Mesopotamia flourished about 6,000 years ago. The Mesopotamians invented the **wheel** and discovered how to make bronze by mixing copper and tin. They also invented a system of **writing**.
Mesopotamian invention was spread by travellers to other parts of the Middle East.

bronze head, probably of Sargon of Agade, found in Assyria and dating from about 2000 BC

metalworking ► page 87

metre *noun*
A metre is the standard unit of length in the **metric system**. In 1791, it was defined as one ten-millionth part of the distance from the North Pole to the Equator. It passed through Dunkirk and Paris in France. There are 100 centimetres in one metre. There are 100 metres in one kilometre.
Distances run and heights jumped in the Olympic Games are measured in metres.

metric system *noun*
The metric system is the system of **weights and measures** now used in every country except the United States of America. It is based on multiples of 10, so that 10 of one unit makes one of the next, higher unit. The metric system was the idea of a French priest, Gabriel Mouton, who suggested it in 1670. It became law in France in 1799.
Using the metric system avoids confusion between one country and another.

metronome *noun*
A metronome is an instrument for beating time in music. It has a **pendulum** which is operated by clockwork and makes a ticking sound at each beat. The timing of the beat can be changed by moving the weight at the end of the pendulum. The metronome's inventor is unknown, but it was first made round about 1800. Some modern metronomes are **electronic**.
A metronome is often used by a pianist learning to play a new piece of music.

microfiche *noun*
A microfiche is a sheet of **film**. It is a store for up to 400 miniature **photographs**. The photographs are viewed by putting the sheet into a microfiche reader. This has a screen on which the magnified images can be seen. **Computer** databases or **compact discs** are taking the place of the microfiche.
Libraries sometimes use microfiches to store details of the books on their shelves.

metalworking   *noun*

Metalworking is the use of metals, such as gold, bronze, iron and steel, for making objects. Bronze was the first metal to be widely used and began the Bronze Age, in about 3500 BC. It is a mixture, or alloy, of copper and tin. The Iron Age started in about 1500 BC. Iron is the most widely used metal today. It is mixed with a small amount of carbon to make steel, which is the most important metal in industry.

Metalworking has produced many useful objects over the centuries.

A blast furnace of the 1500s could heat iron ore to a high enough temperature to melt it.

Bronze Age statue, spearhead and beaker, c. 3000 BC

Henry Bessemer's converter, 1856, produced steel cheaply.

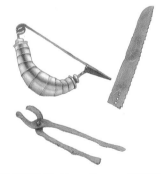

Iron Age brooch, saw and tongs, c. 1000 BC

Hans Christian Oersted of Denmark discovered how to make aluminium in 1825. Aeroplanes are built with aluminium as it is very light and strong.

microfilm *noun*
A microfilm is a roll of **film**. It stores miniature **photographs** in a similar way to the microfiche, and is viewed through a reader. The earliest known microfilm was made in 1852. It was not used widely for record-keeping until the 1920s.
Back issues of newspapers are sometimes stored on microfilm.

micrometer *noun*
A micrometer is an instrument for measuring very small distances and angles. A micrometer calliper has two jaws, like a pair of pliers. The object to be measured is held between the jaws. Astronomical and microscopic micrometers have a filament like a hair which can be moved across the image. The distance the filament moves is shown on a scale.
The astronomical micrometer was invented in 1620 by an Englishman, William Gascoigne.

microphone *noun*
A microphone is an electrical device which changes sound vibrations into electric signals. The signals travel down a wire to an **amplifier** where they are made stronger. The mouthpiece of a **telephone** contains one kind of microphone. The first microphone was made by an English electrician, David Edward Hughes, in 1878.
Microphones are used in radio and television broadcasting.

microprocessor *noun*
A microprocessor is a part of a **computer**. It is a **silicon chip** that makes up the central processing unit. The central processing unit controls the information and programs used by the computer. An American engineer, Jack Kilby, started work on silicon chips in 1958. The first microprocessors were manufactured in 1971 in the United States of America by Intel Corporation.
Many machines in our homes, such as video recorders, contain microprocessors.

microscope *noun*
A microscope is an **optical invention**. It is an instrument for studying very small objects. The simplest light microscope contains one or more **lenses**. These produce an enlarged image of the object being viewed. The light microscope was invented in 1590 by a Dutch glassmaker, Zacharias Janssen. The **electron microscope**, invented in the 1930s, is much more powerful and gives clearer images.
He could see the individual fibres clearly under the microscope.

microwave oven *noun*
A microwave oven is a **cooker**. It uses very short radio waves called microwaves. These make molecules of water in the food vibrate together and produce heat. This cooks the food very quickly. The microwave oven was invented in 1948 by scientists working for the American company Raytheon.
A meal can be prepared in a few minutes using a microwave oven.

milking machine *noun*
A milking machine is a device for milking cows. It has cups which are attached to the cow's teats and connected by hoses to a tank. An electric pump copies the action of a human hand. A milking machine was invented by an American, L. Colvin, in 1862. The first machine to be produced for sale was invented in 1918 by Carl Gustav de Laval in Sweden.
Milking machines save time and labour, and are easily kept clean.

mill *noun*
A mill is a **machine** for grinding grain, such as wheat, into flour between stones or rollers. For thousands of years, grain was ground by hand in stone bowls, or **querns**. The Ancient Chinese were probably the first to use wind power to drive mills. The Ancient Romans built watermills. Most mills today are powered by **electricity**.
In the past, most villages had their own mill where farmers took their grain to be ground.

Miner's Friend *noun*
The Miner's Friend was a **pump** worked by steam. It was used to pump water out of mines. The pump was invented in 1698 by Thomas Savery, an English engineer.
The Miner's Friend was the first steam engine ever built.

mirror *noun*
A mirror is a device which sends back, or reflects, light rays from an object. It presents an image of the object in front of it. Most mirrors are made of glass with a silvered back. This way of making mirrors was invented in Venice, Italy, in about 1320.
The Ancient Egyptians used mirrors made of polished bronze.

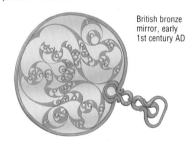

British bronze mirror, early 1st century AD

money *noun*
Money is anything that can be given in exchange for goods or services. It is now usually made of metal or paper.
The Chinese were the first to use paper money, in about AD 800.

monorail *noun*
A monorail is a type of rail transport. It is a **train** that travels on one rail. In some monorail systems, the train hangs below the rail. In others, it runs over it. The first monorail was invented by a British engineer, Henry Robinson Palmer, in 1821. The oldest monorail still in use is an overhead system at Wuppertal in Germany. It was built in 1901.
A monorail carries visitors round Disneyland in California.

Monotype *noun*
A Monotype is a machine which moulds, or casts, type out of metal. The operator sits at a keyboard and types out the letters to be set. This produces a strip of paper tape with a code of holes punched in it. The code tells the casting machine which letters to produce. The Monotype was invented by an American, Tolbert Lanston, in 1887.
Today, electronic typesetting has taken the place of the Monotype.

Morse, Samuel (1791–1872)
Samuel Morse was born in Charleston in the United States of America. He made an **electric telegraph** in 1836 and invented the **Morse code** for use with it. In 1844, a telegraph line was built from Baltimore to Washington. Samuel Morse continued to experiment with telegraphy for the rest of his life.
Samuel Morse was a successful artist before he became interested in telegraphy.

Morse code *noun*

Morse code is an arrangement of dots and dashes which can make up any letter of the alphabet. The dots and dashes can be made by bursts of **electricity** or by flashes of light. A dash is three times as long as a dot. Morse code was invented by an American artist, Samuel Morse, in the late 1830s, for use with the **electric telegraph**.

Morse code was used to send the first telegraph messages across the Atlantic.

mortar *noun*

A mortar is a light gun which fires shells at targets from close range. A shell is dropped down a tube and strikes the firing pin, causing an explosion. The shells move in a high arc so that they can drop behind enemy barricades, or fortifications. The first mortars were very heavy, and were mainly used in sieges. Lighter mortars that could be carried were used in the trench warfare of the First World War.

A mortar fires as quickly as it can be loaded.

European mortar, 1500s

mortice lock *noun*

A mortice lock is a **security** device. It is a lock which fits into the body of a door. This makes it impossible to remove or damage when the door is closed. When the key is turned to close the lock, a bolt moves into a slot cut in a metal plate set in the door frame.

Mortice locks installed in a strong door are very difficult to force open.

motor car *noun*

A motor car is a **road vehicle**. It is powered by an **internal combustion engine**. The inventions that made the motor car possible were by three German engineers. **Nikolaus Otto**, in 1876, invented a gas engine. In 1885, **Gottlieb Daimler** adapted Otto's engine to use petrol. Daimler and **Carl Benz** built motor cars in the same year. Benz used an engine he had built himself.

The first Daimler and Benz motor cars were slow and unreliable.

Otto-Benz three-wheeler, 1888

motor scooter *noun*

A motor scooter is a light-weight **motorcycle** driven by a small petrol engine. It is designed for short journeys in towns and cities. The motor scooter was invented in Italy in the 1950s. One of the best-known makes was Lambretta.

Motor scooters cannot go very fast, but they can weave in and out of traffic.

motorcycle *noun*

A motorcycle is a two-wheeled **vehicle** driven by a petrol engine. It is steered by turning the handlebars. Larger motorcycles can carry a passenger on a seat behind the driver which is called the pillion. **Gottlieb Daimler** made the first motorcycle in 1885, but he decided to concentrate on developing cars instead.

The first company to make motorcycles for sale was Hildebrande and Wolfmüller of Germany in about 1890.

motorway *noun*

Motorway is the name given in the United Kingdom to a high-speed road linking major cities. Motorways have two or more traffic lanes in each direction. In Germany, similar roads are called Autobahn, and in the United States of America they are called superhighways. The first roads of this kind were built in Germany in the 1930s.
The first motorway in the United Kingdom, between London and Birmingham, opened in 1959.

mouse *noun*

A mouse is a device used with a **computer**. It is connected by a wire to the computer and is used instead of a keyboard. A ball underneath the mouse allows it to be moved in any direction. Instructions can be given to the computer by moving the mouse over a desk top or by pressing one or more buttons.
Some computer functions can be carried out faster with a mouse than with a keyboard.

mouth organ *noun*

A mouth organ is a small musical instrument. It contains a number of metal reeds, one for each note. The reeds vibrate when the player sucks or blows into the instrument. Western mouth organs date from the 1820s, and developed from a family of instruments first described in China about 3,000 years ago. Larry Adler, an American living in England, is a famous mouth organ player.
Mouth organs are also called harmonicas.

German mouth organ, c. 1830

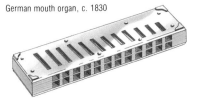

moveable type *noun*

Moveable type is small pieces of wood or metal that are used in **printing**. Each piece carries one letter, number or punctuation mark. When moveable type has been used, the pieces can be split up and used again. Moveable type was a **Chinese invention** of the 1000s. **Johannes Gutenberg**, a German inventor, started printing his first book using moveable type in 1450.
Before moveable type was invented, books had to be copied out by hand.

moving pictures ▶ page 92

mowing machine ▶ lawn mower

musical notation *noun*

Musical notation is the 'language' in which music is written down. European musical notation uses five horizontal lines called a stave on which the notes are arranged. The notes were invented in about AD 700 by Italian monks. The five-line stave, or staff, was developed by Guido of Arezzo in the mid-1000s. Different systems of musical notation are used in many Asian countries. Some of these date back to the Ancient Chinese.
People who understand musical notation are said to be able to 'read music'.

musket *noun*

A musket was a **firearm** which was fired from the shoulder. It was carried by foot soldiers, or infantry. The musket was fired by lighting a charge of **gunpowder** in the barrel. The ammunition was lead shot. Muskets were used from about 1550 to about 1850. After this time, a more powerful firearm, the rifle, was introduced.
The Spanish army was the first to carry muskets.

moving pictures   *plural noun*

Moving pictures describes the images that are put on film and shown on a **television** or **cinema** screen. They are in fact a series of still pictures which follow on from each other very rapidly. This gives the impression of movement. Moving pictures were developed from the **magic lanterns** of the 1700s and 1800s.

With the invention of the video camera in the late 1970s, people can now make their own moving pictures on videotape.

The first successful photographs of movement were of a running horse. British photographer Eadweard Muybridge took the pictures in the late 1870s, using a row of still cameras. Muybridge inspired several inventors to design various types of movie camera and projector in the 1880s.

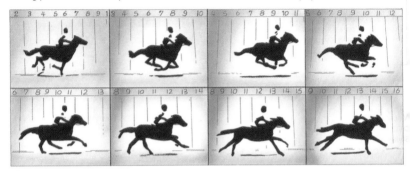

The first commercial cine peep-show was built by Thomas Edison in 1893. It was called the kinetoscope and showed 35-millimetre, black and white films, not enlarged. The viewer looked through a peephole into a large box.

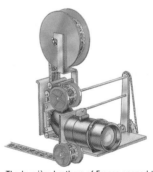

The Lumière brothers of France opened the first cinema in 1895, Their film projector revolutionized film showing as it projected enlarged images onto a screen.

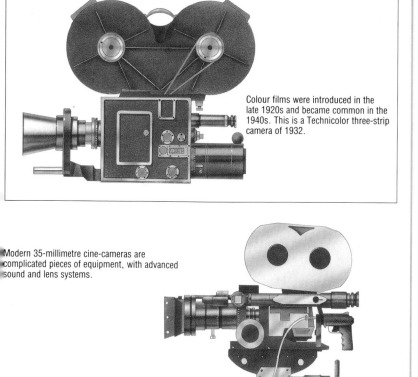

Colour films were introduced in the late 1920s and became common in the 1940s. This is a Technicolor three-strip camera of 1932.

Modern 35-millimetre cine-cameras are complicated pieces of equipment, with advanced sound and lens systems.

Small, hand-held video cameras became available in the 1970s. People could make films at home on videotape and show them on their television screens.

Nobel prizewinner *noun*

A Nobel prizewinner is a man or woman who has won the Nobel Prize for their work. There are six prizes awarded annually — physics, chemistry, physiology or medicine, economics, world peace, literature and economic science. The prize was set up in the late 1800s by **Alfred Nobel**, who was a successful Swedish inventor. The first Nobel prizewinner, in 1901, was **Wilhelm Röntgen**. *In 1903, Marie Curie was the first woman to win the Nobel Prize.*

Alfred Nobel

physics and chemistry

physiology or medicine

Nobel prizewinners receive a gold medal and a cash award. Each of the medals has Nobel's head on one side.

Wilhelm Röntgen

Nobel Prize for Physics, 1901, for discovering X-rays

Marie and Pierre Curie

Nobel Prize for Physics, 1903, for their work on radium

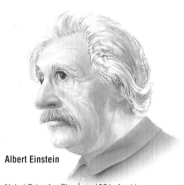

Albert Einstein

Nobel Prize for Physics, 1921, for his
theory of relativity

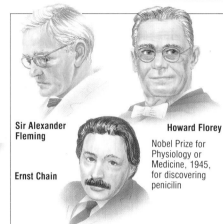

**Sir Alexander
Fleming**

Ernst Chain

Howard Florey

Nobel Prize for
Physiology or
Medicine, 1945,
for discovering
penicilin

Nobel Prize for Physics, 1956, for inventing the transistor

**John
Bardeen**

**William
Shockley**

**Walter
Brattain**

Lev Landau

Nobel Prize for Physics, 1962,
for his research on liquid helium

**Barbara
McClintock**

Nobel Prize for Physiology or Medicine, 1983,
for her work on genetics

nail-making machine *noun*

A nail-making machine is a device that cuts different types of nail from iron sheets or wire. It makes the nail head automatically. Nail-making machines work at great speed. The first machine for making nails out of sheet iron was invented by an American, Jeremiah Wilkinson, in 1775. Another American, William Hassall, invented a machine for cutting nails from wire in 1851.
Before nail-making machines were invented, nails were made by hand.

needle *noun*

A needle is a **tool** for sewing. It has a sharp point at one end and a hole called an eye at the other. A length of thread runs through the eye. Needles made from animal antlers were used over 42,000 years ago. By 3000 BC, metal needles, made of bronze, had been invented. Today, needles are made of steel.
Needles are made in different sizes for different kinds of work.

Newcomen, Thomas (1663–1729)

Thomas Newcomen was born in Devon, England. He worked as a blacksmith and ironmonger. He invented the first successful **steam engine**. Steam power made a vacuum, which sucked down a piston. This raised and lowered a beam which operated a pump. Newcomen's engine was a great improvement on the **Miner's Friend** invented by Thomas Savery. The first Newcomen engine was built at a coal mine in Staffordshire, England, in 1712.
Newcomen engines were used in some British coal mines for over 200 years.

newspaper *noun*

A newspaper is a printed publication. It appears daily or weekly and contains the latest news. The first newspaper was printed in Germany in 1609. The first newspaper in English was published in 1622. The first American newspaper was 'The Boston Newsletter', which started publication in 1704.
Millions of copies of newspapers are sold worldwide every day.

Nissen hut *noun*

A Nissen hut is a building. It is made of sheets of corrugated steel formed into a curve, which makes up the roof and side walls. The end walls are made of wood, brick or stone. Nissen huts can be built quickly by unskilled workers. They were invented by an Englishman, P.N. Nissen, in the 1920s.
Nissen huts are found on many army camps and airfields in the United Kingdom.

Nobel, Alfred Bernhard (1833–1896)

Alfred Bernhard Nobel was born in Stockholm, Sweden. He had little schooling, but learnt five languages while travelling. He spent most of his life studying explosives. In 1867, he patented an explosive which he called **dynamite**. Nobel made a fortune from his inventions. He used the money to set up the Nobel Prizes for physics, chemistry, medicine, literature and peace. These are still awarded each year.
Alfred Nobel invented a detonator which could set off an explosion from a distance.

Nobel prizewinner ► page 94

non-stick pan *noun*
A non-stick pan is a cooking tool. It is a saucepan or frying pan which does not allow food to stick to it during cooking. The inside of the pan is coated with a plastic material called polytetrafluoroethylene, or PTFE. Another name for PTFE is Teflon. PTFE was discovered in 1938, but it was first used for non-stick pans in 1955 by a French scientist, Marc Grégoire.
Non-stick pans are useful for cooking pancakes and omelettes.

nuclear power *noun*
Nuclear power is energy produced by splitting the nucleus of atoms. This is done by bombarding the atoms with particles called neutrons inside a nuclear reactor. The energy released is used to produce steam which drives a **steam turbine**. The turbine generates **electricity**. The first nuclear reactor was built in 1942 in the United States of America by a team led by an Italian scientist, Enrico Fermi.
Many countries rely on nuclear power for part of their electricity supply.

nylon *noun*
Nylon is an artificial fibre. It is used to make fabric for clothes, curtains, furniture coverings and carpets. Nylon is made from chemicals obtained from coal or oil, which are heated to a high temperature. The mixture softens and can be spun into thread. Nylon was first marketed in 1938 by an American chemical firm, Finn Dupont.
Most toothbrushes have bristles made of nylon.

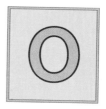

observatory *noun*
An observatory is a place where astronomers study objects in space with the use of large **telescopes**. Optical telescopes observe and record objects in space. Radio telescopes record radio waves from space. The first observatory, long before telescopes were invented, was built in Rhodes, Greece in about 150 BC. Stonehenge, built in England in about 2000 BC, may have been used as an observatory.
The first observatory with a telescope was built in Padua, Italy, in 1610.

odometer *noun*
An odometer is an instrument for measuring the distance travelled by a vehicle. A car's odometer counts the number of turns, or revolutions, made by the **wheels**. From this, the odometer shows the distance travelled in kilometres. The odometer was described by the Roman engineer and architect Vitruvius Marcus Pollio in 25 BC. It was re-invented by Meyneir of France in 1724.
Most cars have an odometer.

Chinese odometer, 1st century AD

offset litho *noun*
Offset litho is a method of **printing**. The text and pictures to be printed are on a plate which is treated so that ink will stick only to certain parts. The ink is then transferred to a rubber roller which in turn prints it on the paper. Litho, or **lithography**, printing was invented by Aloys Senefelder in Germany in 1793. Offset litho has been used only since the 1920s.
Most newspapers are printed by offset litho.

oil painting *noun*
Oil painting is a method of making pictures using colours mixed with linseed oil and varnish. Oil paints were invented by two Flemish brothers, Jan and Hubert van Eyck, in about 1420.
For many years, the van Eyck brothers kept the secret of oil painting to themselves.

oil pipeline *noun*
An oil pipeline is a long pipe. It carries oil from a well to the refinery where it is processed. It also carries oil to a port where it can be shipped. Some oil pipelines run along the sea-bed. They are made by joining together short lengths of steel pipe about one metre in diameter. The Trans-Alaska Pipeline in North America, finished in 1977, is one of the world's longest.
Underwater pipelines are protected from damage by a coating of concrete.

ophthalmoscope *noun*
An ophthalmoscope is an instrument used by doctors and opticians. It is a special kind of electric torch. It shines a beam of light into the eye, so that the back of the eyeball can be examined. This shows up any eye problems. It also gives the doctor an idea of the patient's general health. The ophthalmoscope was invented in 1847 by an Englishman, **Charles Babbage**.
An optician uses an ophthalmoscope when a person has an eye test.

optical invention ► page 99

Otis, Elisha Graves (1811–1861)
Elisha Graves Otis was born in Halifax, in the United States of America. In 1852, he invented a safety device for **elevators**. This allowed passengers as well as goods to travel in elevators. The device was a spring. If the elevator cable broke, the spring flew out and held the elevator safely in place. Otis demonstrated his invention by travelling in an elevator while a mechanic cut the cable.
The first Otis passenger elevator was installed in New York in 1857.

Otto, Nikolaus (1832–1891)
Nikolaus Otto was born in Nassau, Germany. He became an engineer, with little formal training, in 1861. He made the first successful, four-stroke **internal combustion engine**. He used coal gas as a fuel. In 1878, he produced an engine with four cylinders which was developed by **Gottlieb Daimler**.
The actions that take place in a four-stroke engine are still called 'the Otto cycle'.

oven *noun*
An oven is a device for baking food. Over 2,200 years ago, the Ancient Egyptians cooked in clay ovens with a fire inside. By 1780, there were kitchens with enclosed coal fires and ovens at the side. Gas ovens became popular from about 1850, and electric ovens from about 1900. The **microwave oven** was invented in 1948.
The most important use of ovens throughout history has been to bake bread.

optical inventions *noun*

Optical inventions are those inventions that are to do with the eyes and seeing.

Magnifying glasses, spectacles, binoculars, telescopes and microscopes are all optical inventions. They make it easier for a scene or an object to be seen, by bringing it closer and enlarging it or making it clearer.

Contact lenses are an optical invention of the 1900s.

Spectacles

The first spectacles appeared in Italy, in the late 1200s. They were made up of two quartz convex lenses in a frame. They had to be held up to the eyes and could only be used for reading.

Microscopes

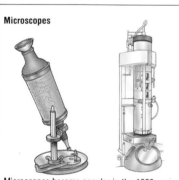

Microscopes became popular in the 1660s, when Robert Hooke of England designed the first example of a modern light telescope. Electron microscopes were invented in 1931 by Max Knoll and E. Ruska of Germany. A modern electron microscope can magnify an object over 1 million times.

Telescopes

Galileo Galilei built a refracting telescope in 1609 that revolutionized the work of astronomers.

Isaac Newton's reflecting telescope of 1668 gave a much clearer image than the early refracting telescopes. It used a system of mirrors.

Huge telescopes are used today in observatories to look deep into space. The main mirror of this reflecting telescope has a diameter of 5.08 metres.

pacemaker *noun*

A pacemaker is an electrical device powered by a battery. It is used by people with certain heart diseases which prevent the heart from beating regularly. The pacemaker sends out electrical impulses which give a regular heartbeat. Pacemakers are implanted under the patient's arm or attached to the chest.
The batteries in pacemakers last up to 30 years before they need to be replaced.

paddle steamer *noun*

A paddle steamer is a form of **water transport**. Its **steam engine** drives two **wheels**, one on each side. The wheels are fitted with paddles which push the boat forward as they push backwards through the water. The sternwheeler has one wheel at the back. The first paddle steamer was built in 1783 by the Frenchman, the Marquis de Jouffroy d'Abbans. An American, Robert Fulton, built the first passenger paddle steamer, called the 'Clermont', in 1807.
In 1819, the paddle steamer 'Savannah' became the first steamship to cross the Atlantic.

padlock *noun*

A padlock is a **security** device. It is a portable lock which can be used wherever it is needed. At the top is a hook. This is opened and hung through a loop, or hasp, on the object to be fastened. Then the hook is closed. The Ancient Chinese used wooden padlocks. Iron padlocks were first used in Europe by the Ancient Romans.
It is a good idea to padlock a bicycle if it is left in a public place.

pantograph *noun*

A pantograph is a drawing instrument. It is used to make copies of designs, maps and drawings. A pantograph consists of pieces of wood or plastic held together loosely with pins. One end is held at the side of the work to be copied. The other end, which holds a **pen** or **pencil**, moves over the work.
Very accurate copies of an original work can be made with a pantograph.

paper *noun*

Paper is a thin material mostly used for **writing** and **printing**. It is usually made from the fibres of plants, such as trees. Paper can also be made from rags of cotton or linen, which are themselves made from plant fibres. Old paper can be used again, or recycled, to make new paper. Paper was invented in China in the 100s BC. It was used for clothing, wrapping parcels and as **lavatory paper**. Fine writing paper was not made until about AD 100.
Most paper today is made from wood pulp.

paper money *noun*

Paper money is a kind of receipt. It can be exchanged for goods or services, or for **coins**. The bank or government which issues paper money promises to pay its value to the owner. Paper money is more convenient than coins to carry and store. It was first used in China around AD 800.
The oldest known European paper money was issued by the Bank of England in 1699.

New Jersey three-shilling note, 1776

paperback book *noun*
A paperback book is a printed publication that has a thick paper cover instead of a stiff, cloth-covered binding. It is less expensive than a hardback book. Small paperback books called chapbooks were sold from about 1700. In the 1890s, railway travellers were able to buy full-length paperback books at stations.
Millions of copies of paperback books are sold every year.

Papin, Denis (1647–c. 1712)
Denis Papin was a French scientist who worked in France, England and Germany. In 1679, he invented a sealed steam vessel with a safety valve. This was the first pressure cooker. It was also the ancestor of the autoclave used to sterilize instruments in hospitals. Denis Papin also had the idea of a steam-driven engine but he had no money to build one.
Denis Papin's skill as an inventor was not rewarded in his time.

parachute *noun*
A parachute is a device for lowering people and objects slowly through the air. It is shaped like an umbrella. Cords lead from the 'envelope' made of silk or nylon to a harness on the wearer's back. When it is closed, the parachute folds into a small pack. **Leonardo da Vinci** designed a parachute in about 1485, but did not make one.
The first parachute jump was made in 1779 from a balloon over Paris.

Paré, Ambroise (1510–1591)
Ambroise Paré was born the son of a barber in Bourg-Hersent, France. He became one of the greatest surgeons in the history of medicine. Paré invented the first **artificial limbs**. These were made of metal, with mechanical joints at the knees, ankles, elbows and wrists. They were held on to the body by a system of belts and straps. Ambroise Paré also played a part in making surgery a recognized profession.
Ambroise Paré believed that bandaging would allow many wounds to heal naturally.

parking meter *noun*
A parking meter is a device found in some city streets. It allows motorists to buy parking time by putting coins or tokens into it. A needle moves across a scale as the time runs out. The parking meter was invented in 1932 by an American, Carl C. Magee.
If motorists leave their car at a meter when the time has run out, they may be fined.

Parsons, Sir Charles (1854–1931)
Sir Charles Parsons was born in London, but spent most of his childhood in Ireland. He was educated at Dublin and Cambridge University and then trained as an engineer. Parsons' most important invention was the **steam turbine**. He first used a steam turbine to generate **electricity** in 1884. His first steam turbine ship, the 'Turbinia', was launched in 1894.
Sir Charles Parsons' steam turbine allowed ships to reach better speeds and save fuel.

Pascal, Blaise (1623–1662)
Blaise Pascal was born in Clermont-Ferrand, France. As a boy, he showed great talent as a mathematician. His most important scientific discoveries were to do with the pressure of liquids and gases. Pascal also invented a mechanical **calculator** in 1642, which used cogged wheels and drums with numbers on them.
Blaise Pascal spent most of his life working on mathematical problems.

passenger railway   *noun*

A passenger railway is a type of rail transport. It is a **railway** for carrying people. People travel by rail to work, to visit their friends and family, on business or on holiday. Some railway **trains** have restaurants and **sleeping cars**. The first passenger railway opened in England in 1825 and ran between the towns of Stockton and Darlington.

America's first passenger railway, the South Carolina Railroad, opened in 1830.

Pasteur, Louis (1822–1895)

Louis Pasteur was born in Dôle, France. He studied chemistry and became a Professor of Chemistry in Strasbourg. Pasteur made many important scientific discoveries. His most famous work was the study of germs and how they spread. He invented a process called **pasteurization**. Pasteur also developed the science of vaccinating animals against deadly diseases.

Louis Pasteur's work led to better understanding of how diseases spread.

pasteurization   *noun*

Pasteurization is a process that is used to preserve certain foods such as milk. The milk is heated, and then cooled quickly to kill any germs that it may contain. This prevents the milk from going sour.

Pasteurization takes its name from Louis Pasteur, who invented the process.

patent   ▶ page 103

pedometer   *noun*

A pedometer is a device carried by a walker. The walker sets the pedometer to measure the length of one step. The pedometer then records the number of steps taken and works out the distance the walker has covered. **Leonardo da Vinci** designed a pedometer in the late 1400s.

A pedometer is strapped to the walker's leg and counts each step.

pen   *noun*

A pen is a **writing** instrument. It has a point called a nib from which ink flows onto the paper. Ancient civilizations used hollow grass stalks or hollow pieces of bamboo. Since the AD 400s, pens called quills have been made of goose feathers. Metal nibs were invented in 1780 by an English manufacturer, Samuel Harrison. The nib had to be dipped in ink for every one or two words.

Pen nibs are made of steel and copy the shape of the quill pen.

pencil   *noun*

A pencil is a **writing** instrument. It is made of wood with a 'lead' in the middle. The lead is made of a mixture of fired graphite and clay. The point is ground with a sharpener. Pencils are made with soft or hard leads for different purposes, such as drawing or writing. A pure graphite pencil was invented by a German, Conrad Gesner, in 1565.

The advantage of using a pencil is that mistakes can be rubbed out with an eraser.

pendulum   *noun*

A pendulum is a weight attached to a wooden or metal rod. The rod is attached to a pivot and this allows the rod to swing freely. The Italian scientist **Galileo** studied the movements of a pendulum in about 1581 and found out how it works. In 1656, a Dutch scientist, **Christian Huygens**, made the first pendulum clock.

The tall case of a grandfather clock has a pendulum inside it.

patent *noun*

A patent is a right granted by a government. It allows an inventor to use and sell an invention. It also prevents other people from stealing the idea. A patent lasts for a certain number of years. In Britain, it lasts for 16 years. After that, anyone may make use of the invention. The earliest known patent granted in England was in 1449. It gave John of Utynam the right to make a certain kind of coloured glass for 20 years.

Anyone who steals the idea of a patent invention may have to pay the inventor.

patent *verb*

Taking out a patent is a lengthy business. At the Patent Office, researchers have to sift through thousands of documents to find out whether something is a new invention or not.

Many forms have to be filled in and fees paid at various stages of registration.

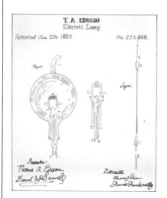

Thomas Edison patented his light bulb on January 27th, 1880.

The Wright brothers patented their flying machine on May 22nd, 1906.

penny-farthing *noun*
A penny-farthing is a kind of **bicycle**. It has a
large front wheel and a very much smaller
back wheel. The saddle is over the front
wheel. It was invented in 1871 by James
Starley, a factory foreman at an English
cycle factory. It was given the name penny-
farthing after the largest and smallest British
copper coins.
*The penny-farthing's proper name was the
ordinary bicycle.*

periscope *noun*
A periscope is an optical device. It allows the
user to see round corners or over obstacles.
It is a tube containing two **mirrors** or prisms.
The object being viewed is reflected from
one mirror or prism onto the second, where it
can be looked at. Submarine crews use
periscopes to look at the surface of the sea.
*The periscope was invented in 1854 in
France, by E.M. Marie-Davy.*

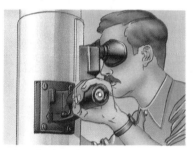

modern submarine periscope

personal computer *noun*
A personal computer is a microcomputer.
It is small enough to stand on a small desk.
The main parts of a personal computer are
a keyboard, control unit and a screen which
is called a monitor or visual display unit.
The first personal computer, the Apple II,
appeared in 1977.
*Personal computers can be linked together
by telephone lines to form a network.*

personal stereo *noun*
A personal stereo is an audio cassette
player. It is small enough to fit into a pocket
or handbag, or hang on a belt. Personal
stereos are powered by **batteries**. A pair of
earphones allows the listener to enjoy tapes
without disturbing other people. The first
personal stereo was the Walkman, made by
the Japanese company Sony in 1979.
*People often listen to personal stereos as
they travel to work.*

petrol pump *noun*
A petrol pump is a **machine** that supplies
road vehicles with petrol or diesel fuel.
An electric **pump** draws fuel from an
underground storage tank. The fuel passes
through a hose and nozzle into the car's fuel
tank. A display on the pump shows the
amount and the price of the petrol taken.
*A trigger mechanism on the nozzle of a
petrol pump turns the supply of petrol on.*

Phoenician invention *noun*
Phoenician invention describes the ideas
and devices that came from the Phoenicians.
The Phoenician civilization flourished from
about 1200 BC to 500 BC, in the area now
called Lebanon. The Phoenicians were great
sailors and explorers. They built the first
merchant **ships**. These were powered by
both sails and oars. The Phoenicians were
the first people to use a written **alphabet**.
*The Phoenician invention of the alphabet
was copied by the Ancient Greeks.*

glass vase, 600 BC

Phoenician alphabet

phonograph *noun*
The phonograph was the first **machine** that **recorded** and reproduced sound. Instead of a **microphone**, it had a diaphragm with a pin mounted on it. Sound made the diaphragm vibrate, and the pin made a groove in a cylinder of tinfoil. The sound was reproduced when the cylinder of tinfoil was replayed. The phonograph was invented in 1877 by the American inventor **Thomas Alva Edison**.
Later versions of the phonograph used wax cylinders instead of tinfoil.

photocopier *noun*
A photocopier is a **machine** that produces copies of paper documents. A bright light reflects the image of the document onto a plate or drum and the image is charged with **electricity**. An ink powder called toner sticks to the charged parts of the image and is transferred onto paper. The photocopier was invented by an American, Chester Carlson, in 1938.
The first colour photocopiers were developed in Japan in the 1970s.

photoflash bulb *noun*
A photoflash bulb is an electronic device used in **photography**. It is a glass tube containing a capacitor which builds up a strong electric current. When this is let out, the tube gives a short burst of bright light. This allows photographs to be taken in dim light or even in the dark. The bulb is operated by a **battery**.
Many cameras have a special socket into which a photoflash bulb can be fitted.

photographic film *noun*
Photographic film is a strip of plastic coated with chemicals. It is used in a **camera**. Photographic film can be bought in rolls or in a cassette. There are many different types and sizes of film. Roll film was invented in 1880 by **George Eastman**. He also invented the Kodak camera to use with it.
Photographic film must be loaded into a camera carefully so it is not exposed to light.

photographic prints ▶ **photography**

photography ▶ page 106

Pi Sheng (c. 1000–c. 1060)
Pi Sheng was a Chinese printer. In 1040, he began **printing** using blocks of **moveable type** made from clay. His invention did not attract much interest, possibly because the clay blocks wore out too quickly. Another problem was the huge number of characters in the Chinese language.
About 400 years after Pi Sheng, Johannes Gutenberg started printing with metal type.

pistol *noun*
A pistol is a light **firearm**. It can be fired at close range with one hand. A pistol is loaded with a bullet. When the pistol is fired, a hammer strikes the end of the cartridge and an explosive drives the bullet out of the muzzle.
The pistol was invented by Caminelleo Vitelli, a gunsmith from Pistoia, Italy, in 1540.

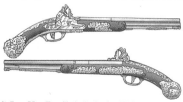

Italian .55 caliber flintlock pistols, 1690

planetarium *noun*
A planetarium is a building in which displays of the night sky are shown. The displays appear on the inside of a domed roof. Below, there are seats for the audience. Moving images of the stars and planets are shone onto the roof by a projector. The first planetarium was opened in Jena, Germany, in 1923 and was designed by a German engineer, Walther Bauersfeld.
In a planetarium, the astronomical events of many years can be viewed in a few minutes.

photography *noun*

Photography is the making of images on film. Light passes through the **lens** of a **camera** onto the film. Chemicals on the film make a negative image. The film is then developed to show a positive image. The first photograph was taken by a French scientist, Joseph Nicéphore Niepce, in 1827. It was printed on metal. An Englishman, **William Henry Fox Talbot**, discovered how to make positive photographic prints from negatives in 1835.

Photography allows parents to keep reminders of their children as they grow up.

camera obscura, early 1800s

Photography as it is known today developed from the camera obscura, which was probably invented in about AD 450, in China. It was a darkened room with a tiny hole in the outside wall. The hole, or later a lens, projected the image of an object or scene onto a screen inside the room.

Some modern automatic cameras have a tiny computer screen on top that gives photographers information about using the cameras.

modern, computerized, fully automatic camera

Eastman's brownie cameras of the early 1900s were cheap and widely available. This reliable, small camera came out in 1925. It used faster film and so the pictures were much clearer.

In 1871, R. Maddox of the UK invented the fast exposure dry plate. In 1888, the American George Eastman developed a small, lightweight camera that used film on a roll.

reliable, small, hand-held camera made by Leitz, 1925

Kodak camera, 1888

first photograph, 1826

The first practical photographic process was invented by L. Daguerre of France in 1839. One print could be made with the first Daguerrotype camera on copper plates coated with silver iodide.

The Frenchman Joseph Nicéphore Niepce was the first to produce a permanent photograph. He coated a pewter plate with a type of asphalt which hardens when it is exposed to light. A faint, permanent image was left on the plate. This is the first photograh ever taken by Niepce.

first Daguerrotype camera, 1839

In 1835, William Fox Talbot of the UK invented the first negative–positive film process. The photographs he took were called calotypes. This picture of Lacock Abbey was taken in 1843. An unlimited number of prints could be made from one negative.

negative–positive calotype of Lacock Abbey, 1843

plastics *plural noun*
Plastics are artificial materials that are not found naturally. They are made in factories by mixing and heating chemicals. There are many different types of plastic. They include **nylon** for clothing, polystyrene for packaging and glass fibre for insulation. The first plastic was made in England in 1855 by Alexander Parkes and was called Parkesite.
Plastics are used to make many articles for the home, such as buckets and bowls.

plastic combs and powder box, 1860s

playing cards ► game

Plimsoll line *noun*
The Plimsoll line is a mark painted on the side of a ship near the waterline. It shows the level to which the ship may be safely loaded. There are different levels for different oceans. The Plimsoll line is named after a British politician, Samuel Plimsoll, who led a campaign for safer shipping. An internationally agreed loading line was adopted by 54 countries in 1930.
Ships must not sail if the Plimsoll line is below water level.

plough *noun*
A plough is a farming **tool**. It is used to turn over the soil before planting seeds. A plough has a curved blade which cuts into the soil and turns it to one side. Ploughs can be pulled along by people, oxen, horses or tractors. The plough was invented in the 7000s to 6000s BC in the Middle East.
Modern ploughs have sharp steel blades.

plumbline *noun*
A plumbline is a simple instrument used by builders. It is a length of cord with a weight on the end. The builder holds one end against a wall and lets the weight hang. This shows whether the wall is vertical. The plumbline was invented in about 800 BC.
A plumbline is also sometimes used by sailors to check the depth of water.

pneumatic drill *noun*
A pneumatic drill is a **tool** for breaking up hard surfaces such as roads. It has a pointed or blade-shaped steel hammer. Compressed air from a **pump** is forced into a cylinder. It pushes down a piston which drives the hammer into the surface. **Blaise Pascal's** discoveries about air pressure in about 1650 helped in the invention of the pneumatic drill.
Pneumatic drills are sometimes called air-hammers or jack-hammers.

Polaroid camera *noun*
A Polaroid camera is a device that takes photographs. The photographs are developed and printed instantly. When a photograph has been taken, the Polaroid camera releases chemicals which develop the photograph in less than a minute. In 1947, an American, Edwin H. Land, invented a Polaroid camera which took black and white pictures. Colour followed in 1963.
Polaroid cameras let you see at once whether you have taken a good photograph.

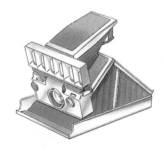

polygraph   *noun*

A polygraph is an electrical instrument. It can detect when people are telling lies. Sensors are placed on a person's body and connected by wires to the polygraph. The sensors pick up body reactions such as changes in pulse rate. These show whether the person is lying when they are asked questions.

The polygraph was invented by a British physiologist, James Mackenzie, in 1882.

porcelain   *noun*

Porcelain is a kind of **pottery**. It is fine, delicate, glazed china that allows light to shine through it. Porcelain is made of white clay which is fired in a very hot kiln. Sometimes, coloured decoration is added before the finished item is glazed. Porcelain is used for tableware and also for ornaments. It was first made in China in about AD 300.

He kept his valuable collection of porcelain locked up in a cabinet.

postage stamp   *noun*

A postage stamp is an adhesive paper label that is used on envelopes. It shows that the sender of the letter has paid to have it delivered. At the post office, the stamp is franked, or marked, so that it cannot be used more than once. The postage stamp was invented by an Englishman, Sir Rowland Hill, in 1840.

Many people collect postage stamps of the world as a hobby.

Penny Black, 1840

postcard   *noun*

A postcard is a piece of thin card that is used for sending short messages by post. Some postcards have a picture on one side. People on holiday often send picture postcards to their friends and family. The first postcards were used in Austria in 1869. Picture postcards began to be popular in the 1890s.

Postcards are often used to invite people to a party.

postcode   *noun*

A postcode is a group of numbers or letters which form part of an address. Postcodes help letters to be sorted more quickly for delivery. In the United Kingdom, postcodes are groups of letters and numbers, for example SN15 1BN. Each postcode stands for a group of addresses, or sometimes for just one address. In most countries, postcodes are made up only of numbers. In the United States of America, they are called zip codes.

People should always use the postcode when they address an envelope.

potato crisp   *noun*

A potato crisp is a thin slice of dried potato fried in oil. Potato crisps are sold in small bags and eaten as snacks. They were first made by the American Indian Chief George Crum, in 1853. Potato crisps were first packed and sold in bags by Frank Smith in England in 1922.

Flavours such as salt, cheese or onion are added to some potato crisps.

potter's wheel   *noun*

A potter's wheel is a machine for making hollow articles out of clay. It is a flat, horizontal **wheel** which is turned by a foot-operated treadle or by an **electric motor**. The potter places a ball of clay on the wheel and moulds the clay as the wheel spins. The potter's wheel was invented in about 3000 BC in Mesopotamia.

Jugs, vases and bowls can all be made on a potter's wheel.

pottery *noun*
Pottery refers to objects made out of clay. The shaped clay is hardened, or fired, by heating. The first potters, in about 9000 BC, shaped clay with their fingers. Hollow objects were made by rolling long strips of clay and coiling them round, smoothing the edges with the fingers. The clay was then dried in the hot sun.
The potters of Ancient Egypt were the first to use ovens called kilns to fire their pottery.

Yugoslavian painted vase, c. 5000 BC

Chinese kettle, c. 4000 BC

Minoan jug, c. 7800 BC

power loom *noun*
A power loom is a machine for **weaving** cloth or carpets. It is driven by an engine or motor. Today's power looms are run by **electric motors** and controlled by **computer** programs. The power loom was invented in 1785 by an English clergyman and inventor, Edmund Cartwright. It was driven by water power.
The power loom was one of the inventions that started the Industrial Revolution.

press stud *noun*
A press stud is a device for fastening clothes. It has two parts. One part is sewn onto each side of the opening to be fastened. A small knob on one part snaps into place in a hole on the other part and is held there until separated. Press studs were invented about 100 years ago.
Press studs are often used to fasten the belts of skirts and trousers.

pressure cooker ► **domestic invention**

pressure suit ► **diving suit**

Priestley, Joseph (1733–1804)
Joseph Priestley was born near Leeds, England. He studied to be a minister, but was also interested in chemistry. Joseph Priestley's scientific work was mainly to do with gases. He discovered how to make **soda water** with carbon dioxide. He found how to make oxygen by heating mercuric oxide. Joseph Priestley also produced other gases such as ammonia, hydrogen chloride and nitrous oxide by passing them through mercury. Priestley's discoveries were used by other inventors.
Joseph Priestley was a keen experimental chemist who kept detailed notes of his work.

printing ► page 112

printing press *noun*
A printing press is a machine for **printing**. A rotary press prints from metal or plastic plates curved round a roller. Paper is fed into the press in separate flat sheets or from a reel. In a photogravure press, an engraved plate or cylinder is used. In an **offset litho** printing press, ink from the plates is passed to a rubber roller before being pressed onto the paper.
The printing works of a newspaper contains a number of printing presses.

propeller *noun*
A propeller is a screw-shaped blade of metal or wood. A shaft joins it to an engine. Propellers are used to drive **ships** and some **aircraft**. As the blade pushes the water or air back, the ship or aircraft is propelled forward. The Greek scientist **Archimedes** discovered that a **screw** could raise water. In 1836, an Englishman and a Swede adapted this idea to make propellers for ships.
Ships often have two or more propellers.

public address system *noun*
A public address system is a means of making announcements or playing music in a large open space. It is made up of sound equipment such as record or cassette players, **microphones** and an **amplifier**. Public address systems are used at concerts, sports events and other large public gatherings.
Public address systems are often used to help control large crowds.

public transport *noun*
Public transport is transport that anyone can use on payment of a fee called a fare. **Trams**, **trains** and **buses** are all forms of public transport. **Stage coaches** provided the first public transport between major cities. They were operating in England by about 1650. Public transport by rail began in England in 1825.
Millions of people travel to work each day by public transport.

stage coach, c. 1650

pulley *noun*
A pulley is a simple **machine**. It is a lifting or pulling device. A rope fits into the grooves on a set of **wheels**. A pull on the rope can lift or pull a heavy weight with little effort. Several pulleys are often used together. This arrangement is called a block and tackle. The first simple pulley, using one wheel, was invented about 3,000 years ago. Pulleys with several wheels were in use by about 300 BC.
Pulleys are used in stores and warehouses to move heavy containers.

pump *noun*
A pump is a **machine** for moving a liquid or a gas. Pumps are used in many different machines and other devices. The Greek inventor Ctesibius made a reciprocating pump for pumping water in the 200s BC. The vacuum pump was invented in 1650 in Germany by **Otto von Guericke**.
Pumps in a car engine deliver petrol and circulate oil and water.

punched cards *plural noun*
Punched cards are a way of giving instructions to a **machine**. Holes punched in certain places on the cards allow the machine to carry out certain actions. A French engineer, Joseph Jacquard, invented the punched card system in 1801. He used it to weave carpet patterns. Punched cards were used to store information in the first **computers**.
Punched cards were used to control machines before computers were invented.

push button *noun*
A push button is a kind of electric switch. When it is pressed, points behind the switch meet and complete an electric circuit. A bell push is a simple example of a push button. Push buttons are also used on many **telephones** and to stop and start **machines**. The keys on the keyboard of a **computer** are push buttons.
Television sets have push buttons which allow different channels to be chosen.

printing *noun*

Printing is a process. It means producing copies of an original picture or text by transferring ink to paper or other material. All the copies are the same. By AD 868, the Chinese were printing books. They carved complete pages of text onto wooden blocks and pressed these onto paper. Printing was re-invented in Europe in 1450, when Johann Gutenberg began using moveable type.

Printing was done by hand-operated presses until steam power was invented.

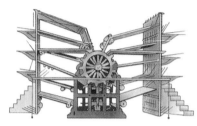

In 1845, Richard Hoe made the first successful rotary press. It was used to print newspapers. A rotary press has a central cylinder with columns of type arranged round it. Rotating cylinders of running paper surround the central one. This type of letterpress printing is still used for newspapers today.

Block printing was probably invented by the Chinese in the AD 500s. The Diamond Sutra of AD 868 is the earliest known printed book, and the earliest example of letterpress printing.

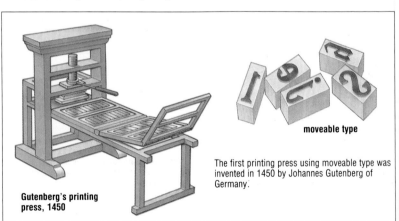

moveable type

Gutenberg's printing press, 1450

The first printing press using moveable type was invented in 1450 by Johannes Gutenberg of Germany.

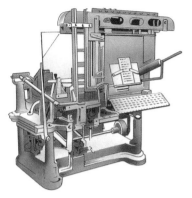

A modern web offset rotary colour press is so large that it fills a room. It can print on both sides of the paper at high speed.

Ottmar Mergenthaler of Germany invented the Linotype composing machine in 1884. The letters were typed on a keyboard and then moulded out of molten metal in a solid line.

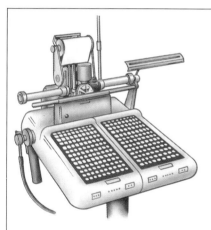

A Monotype typesetting machine was invented in 1887 by T. Lanston of the USA. It cast each letter one after the other. This is a 1950s monotype keyboard.

Most typesetting today is done by computer. A laser scans the text which is then put onto a printing plate photographically.

quartz watch *noun*
A quartz watch or clock is a **timekeeping** device. It contains a crystal of material called quartz. A small **battery** passes an electric current across the quartz. This makes the quartz vibrate, producing a high-frequency electrical signal. The signal is passed to a microchip which activates the watch's hands or digital display. In 1880, two French scientists, Pierre and Jacques Curie, discovered how quartz crystals vibrate. The first quartz watches were made in the 1970s.
Quartz watches and clocks keep very accurate time.

quern *noun*
A quern is a device for making flour from grain. It is made up of two flat, round stones. Grain is placed between them and the top stone is turned, or rotated. A wooden handle can be fixed to the top stone to make it easier to turn. Querns were used thousands of years ago in the Middle East.
Querns are still used in remote villages in some parts of the world.

radar *noun*
Radar is a system that finds the position of distant objects. A radar transmitter sends out radio signals. Some of these are reflected by objects in their path, showing their direction. Their distance is measured by the time the signals take to return. Radar was first demonstrated by a Scottish physicist, Sir Robert Watson-Watt, in 1935.
Radar is used at airports to check the position and speed of approaching aircraft.

radiator *noun*
1. A radiator is part of a **central heating** system. It is made of metal and fitted to the wall or floor of a room. It is heated by hot water flowing through pipes from a **boiler**.
The first radiators were installed in a French country house in 1777.
2. A radiator is part of the cooling system in most cars. It is made up of small pipes and cooling fins. The first **internal combustion engine** fitted with a radiator was built by an Austrian engineer, Siegfried Marcus, in 1864.
The radiator is found at the front of the car behind a grille.

radio *noun*
Radio is a form of **broadcasting**. Radio transmitters send out information on electromagnetic waves. A radio receiver collects the waves and changes them back into sound. The first radio signals were sent by an Italian inventor, **Guglielmo Marconi**, in 1895. The first sound broadcast was made in 1906 by a Canadian, Reginald Fessenden.
Radio is a major source of information and entertainment throughout the world.

radio telescope *noun*
A radio telescope is an instrument used by
astronomers. It picks up and strengthens, or
amplifies, radio signals given out by objects
in the sky. The signals are collected by a
large dish aerial which can be turned in any
direction. From the signals, radio
astronomers can make radio maps of outer
space. An American astronomer, Grote
Reber, built the first radio telescope in 1937.
*Radio telescopes can pick up signals from
stars which are too distant to be seen.*

Mark 1A radio telescope, Jodrell Bank, UK

raft *noun*
A raft is a craft which travels on water.
It is made up of logs or bundles of reeds
fastened together to make a flat platform. A
raft floats on the surface of the water. Some
rafts are pushed along with paddles or with a
long pole. Others are fitted with a sail. Rafts
were used thousands of years ago, long
before people had learned to build boats.
*A famous explorer, Thor Heyerdahl, sailed
across the Pacific Ocean on a raft.*

rail *noun*
A rail is a length of iron, steel or wood. Rails
are laid end to end to make a track. Before
the **steam locomotive** was invented, rails
were used to make a smooth track for horse-
drawn **wagons**. They were laid above and
below ground in coal mines, and at docks.
Steel rails were developed in the 1860s.
*Ancient peoples used lengths of wooden rail
to move heavy rocks for building.*

railway ▶ page 116

railway carriage *noun*
A railway carriage is a **vehicle** designed to
carry passengers by rail. Some railway
carriages contain restaurants and bars.
Some, called **sleeping cars**, have bunk
beds for passengers to sleep in. The first
railway carriages were used at the opening
of the Stockton to Darlington Railway in
England in 1825.
*The first railway carriages were simple coal
wagons fitted with benches.*

'Rocket' carriage, 1829

railway points *noun*
Railway points are devices that allow **trains**
to change tracks. Points are made up of
short lengths of **rail**. They can be moved so
that they fit tightly against the fixed rails of
two other tracks. Points were invented when
the first long-distance **railways** were built in
the 1830s. They were set by moving a **lever**
beside the track.
*Today, railway points are set electrically
from signal boxes often miles away.*

railway signals *noun*
Railway signals are sets of moveable metal
arms or coloured lights. They show a train-
driver whether the track ahead is clear. The
first mechanical signal was a flag that was
turned at right angles to the track to stop a
train. Today, most signals are coloured lights
similar to **traffic lights**.
*The first railway signal was used on the
Liverpool and Manchester Railway in 1834.*

115

railway *noun*

A railway is a system of transport. It can carry freight or passengers in trains of wagons or carriages drawn by locomotives. The Liverpool and Manchester Railway was the first to use steam locomotives for carrying both freight and passengers. It was opened in 1830.

The first railways were built mainly to carry heavy freight such as coal and building stone.

The first railway locomotives were powered by steam. Richard Trevithick of England built the first steam engine in 1804.

The first electric railway was opened in Germany in 1879. A modern electric locomotive picks up electricity from overhead wires. France's electric TGV trains are the fastest trains in the world, running at a top speed of 300 kph.

The first successful diesel-electric locomotive developed in America, in 1923. Diesel-electric diesel, and electric locomotives have replaced steam in most countries today. The railway of future may be the magnetic levitation train, or maglev for short.

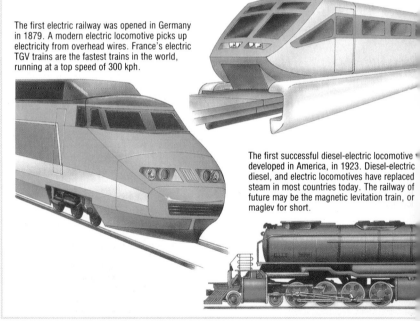

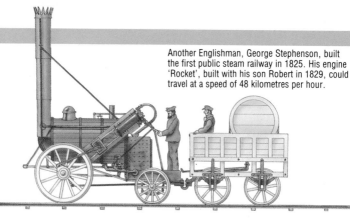

Another Englishman, George Stephenson, built the first public steam railway in 1825. His engine 'Rocket', built with his son Robert in 1829, could travel at a speed of 48 kilometres per hour.

The first underground railway opened in London in 1863. It used steam locomotives. Electric tube trains were first built in 1890.

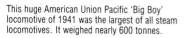

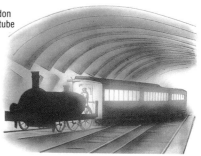

By 1938, a steam locomotive called 'Mallard' had set a world speed record of 202 kph.

This huge American Union Pacific 'Big Boy' locomotive of 1941 was the largest of all steam locomotives. It weighed nearly 600 tonnes.

raincoat *noun*

A raincoat is an overcoat made of waterproof material. The spaces between the fibres of the material are sealed so that rain cannot soak through them. A raincoat is sometimes called a macintosh. It takes this name from Charles Macintosh, a Scottish chemist who invented waterproof material in 1823.
Raincoats sometimes have two thicknesses of material over the shoulders.

rayon *noun*

Rayon is an artificial fibre. It is made from wood pulp dissolved in chemicals. This produces tiny threads, or filaments, which can be spun into yarn. Rayon yarn is woven into fabric. The process was invented in 1884 by a French scientist, Hilaire de Chardonnet. The word 'rayon' was first used in the United States of America in 1924.
Rayon has a silky feel and was once called artificial silk.

razor *noun*

A razor is a device for removing hair from the skin. Until about 100 years ago, open razors were used. These had a sharp blade attached to a handle. In 1901, an American, **King C. Gillette**, invented the safety razor. This has a thin steel blade protected by a guard. The electric razor or shaver, powered by an **electric motor**, was invented in 1928 in the United States of America by Jacob Schick.
The blade of a safety razor can be removed and replaced when it has lost its sharpness.

Gillette safety razor, 1901

reaper *noun*

A reaper is a machine for cutting wheat. It has rotating blades which lift the wheat into a position for cutting. The wheat is then separated from the stalks by a knife which moves backwards and forwards. A successful early mechanical reaper was built by **Cyrus Hall McCormick** in 1831. Early reapers were drawn by horses.
Today, the reaper is part of a combine harvester, which carries out all the tasks of harvesting.

rear-view mirror *noun*

A rear-view mirror is a device that is fitted inside a **motor car** or on a front door frame. It allows people to see what is happening behind them. A rear-view mirror in a car is often curved outwards, or convex, so that the driver has a wide-angled view of traffic behind. The mirror can be adjusted for drivers of different heights.
Some rear-view mirrors can be adjusted so that the driver is not dazzled at night.

Réaumur, René-Antoine Ferchault de (1683–1757)

René-Antoine Ferchault de Réaumur was born in Rochelle, France. He was a scientist who did research in many different fields, including the study of insects. He invented a **thermometer** in which a column of alcohol showed the temperature. He also invented the Réaumur **temperature scale**. On this scale, 80 degrees separate the freezing and boiling points of water. The Réaumur scale is no longer used.
Réaumur's other inventions included the first opaque glass, which meant it could not be seen through.

record ► gramophone record

recording ► page 120

refrigeration ► page 122

refrigerator ► refrigeration

respirator *noun*
A respirator is a kind of breathing apparatus. It is a mask that fits tightly to the face with straps over the head. A respirator has an eyepiece through which the wearer can see. The wearer breathes in, either through a chemical pad, or from a separate supply of oxygen carried on the chest or back. Respirators are used to avoid breathing in gas or dangerous fumes. A charcoal respirator was invented in 1854 by Dr John Stenhouse. An oxygen respirator was invented in 1870 by Dr John Tyndall.
Respirators are often used in hospitals to supply oxygen to patients.

revolver *noun*
A revolver is a kind of **pistol**. It has a revolving cylinder carrying several cartridges. This allows it to fire a number of shots without reloading. The revolver was invented in 1835 by an American, Samuel Colt.
Colt revolvers were first used by the American army in 1846.

revolving door *noun*
A revolving door is a device that is found at the front of many offices and hotels. It is made up of four doors that are joined and pivoted at one end. They turn, or revolve, inside a circular porch. There are no locks or handles. Revolving doors can easily be used by people carrying heavy luggage, as their hands can be left free.
Revolving doors keep out draughts because they are never open.

revolving stage *noun*
A revolving stage is part of the equipment of many theatres. The floor of the stage is fixed to a pivot in the centre. A new scene can be shown to the audience without a break, while the previous scene is changed. Modern revolving stages are operated by an **electric motor**. The revolving stage was invented in Japan in about 1760.
Musical shows often use a revolving stage for quick changes of scene.

Richter Scale *noun*
The Richter Scale is a measurement of the strength, or intensity, of earthquakes. Vibrations through the Earth's crust are recorded on a **seismograph**. A force 1 earthquake on the Richter Scale causes a slight tremor but no damage. A force 7 earthquake causes a major disaster. The Richter Scale was invented in 1935 by the American Charles Richter.
Each Richter Scale number indicates a force ten times stronger than the previous one.

rifle *noun*
A rifle is a **firearm**. The inside of its barrel has a spiral groove running from back to front. The groove makes a bullet spin as it is fired and increases its range and power. The first rifles were made in the late 1400s.
From about 1850, most armies equipped their foot soldiers with rifles.

road *noun*
A road is a track with a hard surface. Today, roads designed for cars and trucks have a surface of concrete or tarmac. They have curved, or cambered, surfaces so that water drains off. In many countries, only the main roads between major cities have these surfaces. Early roads were built soon after the **wheel** was invented in about 3000 BC.
The Romans built a large number of long, straight roads.

Roman road-builders, 200 BC

119

recording *noun*

Recording is the setting down of sounds onto paper, tape or disc. The first recording was made by **Thomas Edison** in 1877. He recorded the word 'hello' as indentations on paper, using a telephone repeater. The first magnetic recording was made by the Danish inventor Valdemar Poulsen in 1898. He used steel piano wire. Plastic tape was invented in 1935.

The first recording on disc was made by Emile Berliner in 1887 for his gramophone.
record *verb*

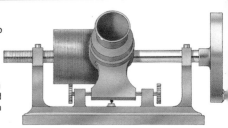

Edison's phonograph, 1877

Tape recording

The first magnetic recorder made recordings on steel piano wire. In 1928, F. Pfleumer of Germany invented magnetic tape. It was made of paper coated with magnetic particles. The cassette recorder was introduced in 1963, made by Philips.

Poulsen's telegraphone, 1903

cassette recorder, 1963

Berliner's gramophone, 1888

Disc recording

The first metal disc, or record, and record player were invented in 1887 by Emile Berliner. He introduced shellac discs in 1895. These were used until 1948, when the vinyl long-playing record was introduced. Scratch-resistant compact discs have now largely replaced LPs.

Edison's gramophone, 1905, with a sapphire stylus

modern compact disc player

78 rpm shellac record

long-playing vinyl record

compact disc

refrigeration *noun*

Refrigeration is a way of cooling things. It moves heat from one place to another. Refrigeration helps to preserve food and keep it fresh for longer. Storing food on ice is an ancient method of refrigeration. Mechanical refrigeration was not invented until the mid–1800s. A British-born engineer, John Harrison, set up refrigeration machines in a brewery in Australia. Refrigeration in the home did not begin until 1879.

Refrigeration of food is especially important in hot countries.

The first domestic electric refrigerator was designed in 1923 by B. von Platen and C. Munters of Sweden. This one was made in 1927.

A mechanical refrigerator of 1903 used ammonia as the cooling liquid, or refrigerant.

A modern refrigerator has a condenser and a compressor. Freon gas is pumped by the compressor to the condenser where it changes into liquid. This cools the refrigerator.

road vehicle ▶ page 124

robot *noun*
A robot is a machine that can perform a wide range of tasks. It copies the actions of a human. Robots controlled by computer programs perform tasks such as putting motor car bodies together. The word 'robot' was first used in 1920 in a play by a Czech dramatist, Karel Capek. Robot tools were first used in a Japanese factory, in 1970.
Robots are used to perform tasks that humans would find boring or dangerous.

rocket *noun*
A rocket is a device powered by explosive gases. It contains chemicals which burn to produce a powerful force. This pushes the rocket upwards or forwards. Rockets used to put spacecraft or **satellites** into space are fuelled by hydrogen and oxygen under great pressure. Rockets were a **Chinese invention**. By about 1150, the Chinese were using rockets powered by **gunpowder**.
The first liquid-fuel rocket was launched by an American, Robert H. Goddard, in 1926.

rocket car *noun*
A rocket car is a **motor car** powered by a rocket engine. Rocket engines produce far more energy than the highest-powered **internal combustion engine**. Rocket cars can reach high speeds, but cannot keep them up for long before the fuel runs out. In the 1930s, a German engineer, Max Valier, experimented with many rocket cars.
The rocket car was an invention which had no practical use.

'Blue Flame', 1970, world speed record of 1,014 kph

roll film ▶ **photographic film**

roller bearings *plural noun*
Roller bearings are parts of some **machines**. They fit between the moving parts of a machine and allow them to move smoothly and easily. A roller bearing is made of steel. It usually has an inner and an outer ring with a space between them. A roller fits into the cylinder-shaped space. It is free to roll as the two parts of the machine move. Roller bearings were first used in the late 1700s.
Roller bearings are oiled to reduce rubbing, or friction.

roller skates *plural noun*
Roller skates are platforms or boots on wheels. They allow people to move over hard surfaces with very little effort. Each platform is fitted with four wooden, metal or plastic rollers that can move freely. Roller skates are attached to the feet with straps. Wheeled skates were used in the Netherlands in the 1700s. Modern roller skates were invented in 1863 by an American, J.L. Plimpton.
Racing on roller skates was a popular sport 100 years ago.

wooden roller-skates, 1780

Roman invention *noun*
Roman invention describes the ideas, tools and machines that came from the Ancient Romans between about 40 BC and AD 400. Roman inventions included the Latin **alphabet**, hot-air **central heating** and a **crane** powered by a treadmill.
Hot baths, using a furnace below a cistern, were a Roman invention.

road vehicle *noun*

A road vehicle is any means of carrying,
or transporting, goods or people by road.
Bicycles, carts, buses and cars are all road
vehicles. The history of road vehicles began
with the invention of the **wheel** about 5,000
years ago. More and more complicated
vehicles were developed, but they were only
as fast as the people or animals that pulled
them. Faster road vehicles were possible
after the invention of the **internal
combustion engine**.

*The fastest road vehicles are some sports
cars that can travel at speeds of up to
288 kilometres per hour.*

two-wheeled cart drawn by oxen, 2000 BC

first practical motorcycle, Hildebrand and
Wolfmüller, 1894

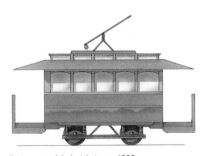

first successful electric tram, 1888

Benz carriage, 1885 — first vehicle powered by a
four-stroke petrol engine

Chinese wheelbarrow, AD 200s

Two inventions have been especially important for the development of road transport. These were the invention of the wheel and, thousands of years later, the invention of the internal combusion engine.

Trams were used as early as 1775, but they were puled by horses. Primitive bicycles were pictured by the Ancient Chinese and Egyptians. But there is no evidence that they were built and used. The first motorcycle was a two-wheeled, wooden machine built in 1885 by two Germans, Wilhelm Maybeck and Gottlieb Daimler.

four-wheeled Celtic ceremonial wagon, AD 100

horse-drawn stage coach, 1650

penny-farthing bicycle, 1870s

first steam-powered road vehicle, 1769

rope   *noun*
Rope is a length of strong material used for hanging, pulling and tying objects. It is made by twisting together animal, vegetable or artificial fibres into strands and then weaving the strands together. Rope was one of the first inventions and was used over 10,000 years ago.
Rope is still made by hand from hemp fibres.

roof tile   *noun*
A roof tile is a rectangular piece of baked clay or concrete. Roof tiles are used to protect a building from the weather. They are nailed to a wooden framework that forms part of the roof timbers. Roof tiles are designed to overlap so that rain does not get between them. They were used by the Ancient Greeks and probably in earlier civilizations.
Builders often put a layer of roofing felt under roof tiles to give extra protection.

Ancient Greek roof tiles, c. 700s BC

rotary ventilation fan   *noun*
A rotary ventilation fan is a cooling device. It helps to circulate the air in a room. It is made up of a number of curved blades mounted on a shaft. The shaft is driven by an **electric motor**. Many rotary ventilation fans move round in an arc so that they ventilate a larger area of the room. Ventilation helps to make people in a hot or stuffy atmosphere feel more comfortable.
Large rotary ventilation fans are sometimes fitted to the ceilings of rooms.

rubber boots   *plural noun*
Rubber boots are a type of waterproof footwear. They are used when the ground is wet or muddy. Each boot is made in one piece. Rubber boots have no laces or other fastenings. They stay on because they are tight at the ankle and come up almost to the knee. The first rubber boots were made in the United States of America in the 1840s.
Rubber boots are lined with fabric and sometimes with nylon fur.

rubber tyre   *noun*
A rubber tyre is a part of a **vehicle**. It covers the outer edge of the wheels. **Road vehicle** tyres are pneumatic. The outer casing of rubber contains air under pressure. The pneumatic tyre was invented by a Scotsman, Robert Thomson, in 1846. Solid rubber tyres were also invented in the 1840s.
Pneumatic rubber tyres must be kept inflated to the correct air pressure.

rubber vulcanization   *noun*
Rubber vulcanization is a manufacturing process. Latex from rubber trees is heated with sulphur and other chemicals to make a plastic mixture. This can be moulded into various products. The process of vulcanization was invented by an American, Charles Goodyear, in 1839.
Goodyear's invention of rubber vulcanization was the start of the rubber industry.

rudder   *noun*
A rudder is part of the steering mechanism of a **ship** or **aircraft**. A ship's rudder is a flat piece of wood or metal which sticks out, or projects, from the stern. An aircraft rudder is part of the tail unit. A rudder can be moved to the left or right, in the direction opposite to the direction of travel. The rudder was a **Chinese invention** of the first century AD.
In a modern ship, the rudder is controlled electrically from the bridge.

saddle *noun*
A saddle is a seat for a rider on a horse's back. A saddle is made of leather and is strapped to the horse with a wide belt, or girth. The **stirrups** hang from the saddle, one on either side. The first saddles were merely folded blankets. Leather saddles probably appeared in China about 100 BC. The western-type saddle has a deep seat for cattle-roping, while the English-type saddle is light and flat, and used for sport.
Saddles were used by cavalry soldiers to give them a firm seat during battles.

safety belt *noun*
A safety belt is a device that protects travellers in aircraft and cars. It is made of strong material called webbing that can cope with strain. Aircraft safety belts are worn during take-off and landing. Car safety belts are worn whenever the car is moving. They were first used in the late 1960s.
A safety belt has a simple but strong lock that can be fastened or unfastened quickly.

safety curtain *noun*
A safety curtain is a **security** device found in a theatre. It is a fireproof sheet that can be lowered to separate the stage from the audience. Safety curtains were introduced after a series of disasters when fire spread from the stage to the rest of the theatre. The first was put in place at Drury Lane Theatre in London, in 1794.
In the United Kingdom, the safety curtain is tested at each performance to make sure it is working properly.

safety glass *noun*
Safety glass is a special type of **glass** that does not splinter if it is broken. Early safety glass was strengthened with wire mesh. It was first made in Germany by the Siemens company in 1891. Laminated glass was invented in 1905. It is made up of a 'sandwich' of two sheets of glass with clear plastic between. If it is broken, the pieces of glass are held together by the plastic.
Safety glass may also be made by heating glass sheets, then cooling them.

safety lamp *noun*
A safety lamp was a form of **lighting**. It was a **lamp** that was used in coal mines before electric lamps were invented. It had a body made of wire gauze surrounding an oil lamp. The gauze stopped the flame setting light to gas in the air and causing an explosion. A safety lamp was invented in 1815 by both **Humphry Davy**, a British scientist, and **George Stephenson**, a British engineer.
Safety lamps could detect explosive gas, which made the flame change colour.

safety pin *noun*
A safety pin is a fastener for clothes. It is made of metal. A safety pin has a guard covering the point of the pin to stop it pricking the wearer. Iron safety pins were in use in southern Europe from about 1300 BC.
The modern safety pin was invented in 1849 by the American, Walter Hunt.

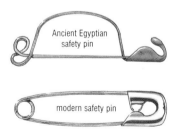

Ancient Egyptian safety pin

modern safety pin

safety razor ► **razor**

sandwich *noun*
A sandwich is a type of food. It is made of two slices of bread with a filling between them. It is a nourishing snack for people who are unable to stop for a proper meal. The sandwich was named after a British statesman, the Earl of Sandwich, in about 1750. He wanted to eat without interrupting his favourite pastime, gambling.
It is interesting to try out new fillings for sandwiches.

satellite *noun*
A satellite is an object that is travelling, or is in orbit, around another object in space. Artificial satellites have been placed in orbit round the Earth. These satellites can receive and send radio signals from and to Earth. The first artificial satellite was Sputnik I, which was launched from the former Soviet Union in 1957.
Satellites are launched into orbit by rockets.

Savery, Thomas (c. 1650–1715)
Thomas Savery was born in Shilstone, in England. He worked as a military engineer. The most famous of his inventions was the **Miner's Friend**, built in 1698. This was the first steam-operated engine for pumping water from mines. His other inventions included a **pump** for supplying water to the fountains of the royal palace at Hampton Court near London.
Thomas Savery's Miner's Friend was soon followed by the more efficient Newcomen engine.

saw *noun*
A saw is a **tool** for cutting wood or metal. It has a handle and a blade with a toothed edge. It is worked by drawing the blade across the material to be cut. Hand saws are still used, but many saws today are powered by petrol or electric motors. The Ancient Romans used saws which had blades made of bronze.
Saws with specially hardened blades for cutting metal are called hacksaws.

saxophone *noun*
A saxophone is a musical instrument. Its mouthpiece has a single reed like that of a clarinet, but its body is brass instead of wood. Saxophones are often heard in jazz bands. The saxophone was invented in the 1840s by Adolphe Sax, a Belgian instrument-maker who lived in France.
The composer Richard Strauss wrote a symphony with parts for four saxophones.

scales *plural noun*
Scales are **machines** for measuring weight. The simplest kind of scales is the beam balance. This is a length of wood or metal either hanging on a cord, or balanced on a central pivot. An object to be weighed is hung from one end of the beam. A known weight is hung at the other end. The beam balance was used in Ancient Egypt about 7,000 years ago.
Electronic scales show the result on a display.

scissors *plural noun*
Scissors are a cutting **tool**. They are a kind of **lever**. Scissors are made up of two sharp steel blades. The blades are held together by a **screw**, which acts as the pivot. When the handles are operated by a finger and thumb, the blades meet and cut the material between them. Pivoted scissors made of iron were used by the Ancient Romans.
Scissors are used for many every-day jobs, such as cutting hair and trimming nails.

scooter ▶ motor scooter

screw *noun*
1. A screw is a type of simple **machine**. It has an inclined plane winding in a spiral along its length. In Ancient Greece, **Archimedes** used the idea of the screw to raise water from one level to another.
The screw can be put to many different uses.
2. A screw is a metal fastener used mainly for wood. A spiral ridge called a thread runs from the point to the head. The head has a slot cut into it so that the screw can be turned by a **screwdriver**.
Screws are made from brass or steel.

screw-down tap *noun*
A screw-down tap is a device that controls the flow of water from a pipe. There is a rubber washer inside the tap. When the handle is screwed down, the washer forms a seal and prevents water from dripping through. Turning the handle the other way releases the washer and lets the water flow.
The washer in a screw-down tap must be replaced if it allows the tap to drip.

screwdriver *noun*
A screwdriver is a tool for driving **screws** in or out of objects. A metal blade fits into a wooden or plastic handle. The tip of the blade fits into a slot or cross on the head of the screw, and the handle is used to turn it. Short screwdrivers called turnscrews were used from about 1550.
The modern screwdriver with a long blade was invented in 1780.

seaplane *noun*
A seaplane is an **aircraft** that has floats instead of wheels on its undercarriage. It is designed to land on and take off from water. The first practical seaplane was built in 1911 by the American designer, Glenn Curtiss.
Many seaplanes were built in the 1920s and 1930s, but few are built today.

security ▶ page 130

seed drill ▶ agricultural machinery

seismograph *noun*
A seismograph is an instrument for measuring the force of tremors in the Earth's crust. It is used to record earthquakes and to find oil supplies underground. Modern seismographs can record tremors on electronic screens. The first seismograph was a mechanical device using a **pendulum**. It was invented in AD 132 in China by Chang Heng.
Seismographs can record the time and direction of a tremor as well as its force.

model of Chang Heng's seismograph

semaphore *noun*
Semaphore is a method of **communicating** over a distance, using flags or pointers to send signals. Before the **electric telegraph** and radio were invented, semaphore was used for communications between army units and ships. The system was invented in the 1790s by a Frenchman, Claude Chappe.
The word 'telegraph' was first used to describe the semaphore system.

security *noun*

Security is the feeling or state of being safe. It is freedom from danger, fear or care. People have always wanted to keep themselves and their possessions secure. In very early times, they had no means of locking their dwellings. But they could dig a hole to put things in and cover it with a stone. The first key-operated lock was invented in Ancient Egypt in about 2000 BC.

Today, security may take the form of electronic locks that open after reading a code.

Russian padlock, 1500s

padlock

key

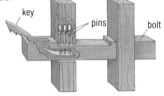

Ancient Egyptian wooden lock

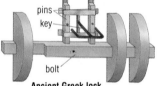

Ancient Greek lock

In this Dutch lock of the 1600s, pushing a secret button makes the man's leg kick up to reveal the keyhole. The lock bolt can be released by pushing back his hat.

modern cylinder lock

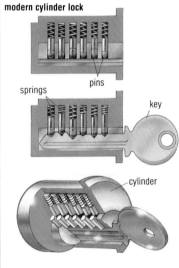

In 1848, Linus Yale invented the modern cylinder lock, which is now known as the Yale lock. It is used to secure most house doors and car doors.

semiconductor *noun*

A semiconductor is a piece of crystal. It is used to control the flow of **electricity** in electrical devices. Semiconductors are used to make **diodes** and **transistors**. In diodes, electric current can flow in only one direction. In transistors, the current can be made stronger. Semiconductors were invented in 1948 by three American scientists,•William Shockley, John Bardeen and Walter Brattain.
Semiconductors are used in electronic devices.

sewing-machine *noun*

A sewing-machine is a device for automatic needlework. Early machines were worked by turning a handle or operating a treadle. The first sewing-machine was made by a French tailor, Barthélémy Thimmonier, in 1830. Sewing-machines for home use were developed in the United States of America by Elias Howe, in 1846, and Isaac Singer, in 1851.
Most sewing-machines today have electric motors.

Elias Howe's
sewing-machine

sextant *noun*

A sextant is an instrument for finding **latitude**. It consists of a **lens**, a set of **mirrors** and a scale. The user points the lens at the horizon and adjusts the mirrors until a faint image of the Sun appears on it. The angle between the Sun and the horizon is read from the scale. From this, the latitude can be worked out.
The sextant was invented in 1757 by an Englishman, Captain John Campbell.

shadoof *noun*

A shadoof, or shaduf, is a **machine** for raising water for **irrigation**. It works in a similar way to a see-saw. A shadoof is a beam balanced on a pivot or fulcrum. At one end, there is a heavy weight. At the other end, there is a container which is filled with water. A light pull on the beam allows the water to be raised.
The shadoof was invented at least 7,000 years ago.

sheep-shearing machine *noun*

A sheep-shearing machine is a device for removing the fleeces of sheep. It is powered by an **electric motor**. A comb lifts the sheep's wool and sharp blades pass to and fro across it.
Sheep-shearing machines have replaced hand-shears for clipping sheep.

shellac *noun*

Shellac is a natural **plastic** material. It is made from resin produced by certain insects. Artificial plastics are now used instead of shellac. **Gramophone records** were once made of shellac but are now made of vinyl.
Shellac was once used to make high-quality varnish for furniture.

ship *noun*

A ship is a large, sea-going vessel. The first people to build ships were the Egyptians, in the 3000s BC. They invented sails and built ships out of planks of wood. Egyptian ships were powered by both sails and oarsmen.
The Minoans of Crete made the first large, sea-going ships, as early as 2500 BC.

shop *noun*

A shop is a place where goods are exchanged for **money**. The first shops were stalls in open-air markets or bazaars. Ancient Roman cities had permanent shops. Today, shops are grouped in the centres of towns and cities, and on main roads on the outskirts.
Shops in Ancient Rome attracted customers by their displays of goods for sale.

shorthand   *noun*
Shorthand is a system of rapid **writing**. It is used for making notes of the spoken word. The symbols used in shorthand can be made more quickly than the ordinary alphabet. A Roman citizen, Marcus Tullius Tiro, invented a system of shorthand in 63 BC. In English-speaking countries, the system invented by Isaac Pitman in 1837 is still used.
Shorthand is sometimes called stenography.

silicon chip   *noun*
A silicon chip is a thin wafer of a material called silicon. It is about five millimetres square. On each chip is a network of thousands of transistors and other parts. Silicon chips are used in electronic equipment. The term 'silicon chip' was used from the 1960s for a device invented in 1958 by an American engineer, Jack Kilby.
Silicon chips are also called integrated circuits.

Singer, Isaac Merrit   (1811–1875)
Isaac Merrit Singer was born in Oswego, New York, in the United States of America. He was the inventor of an early **sewing-machine**. His 1851 machine was not the first, but Singer was a skilful salesman and saw that there was a market for domestic sewing-machines. He made it easier for people to buy the machines by introducing payments by instalment, or hire purchase.
Isaac Merrit Singer's company had sold over 110,000 machines by 1869.

skates   ► ice skates and roller skates

skis   *plural noun*
Skis are long, narrow runners attached to the feet. They are used for travelling over snow. Their running surfaces are made of polished wood, metal or plastic. Skis are worn with heavy boots. Skiers use two poles to help them steer and balance. Leather skis were used by the Norse peoples around 2000 BC. Skiing as a sport began in Norway in 1860.
Skis have quick-release bindings so they drop away from the boots if the skier falls.

skis in Swedish rock carving of about 2000 BC

skyscraper   *noun*
A skyscraper is a tall building with many storeys. Most skyscrapers are built on frames of steel girders which carry the weight of the building. The first skyscraper built in this way was the Home Insurance Building in Chicago, United States of America. It was designed by the American architect William Jenney and built in 1885.
The tallest skyscraper in the world is the Sears Tower in Chicago, 110 storeys high.

sleeping car   *noun*
A sleeping car is a **railway carriage** in which passengers can sleep on bunk beds. The first sleeping cars, called bed-carriages, ran on the London and Birmingham Railway in England from 1838. In 1859, an American engineer, George Mortimer Pullman, invented the luxury Pullman sleeping car.
Rail travel by sleeping car used to be popular in the USA.

slide rule *noun*

A slide rule is a mathematical instrument. It has a number of slides with number scales printed on them. These slides can be moved to carry out calculations. The slide rule was invented by an Englishman, William Oughtred, in 1621. In the 1970s, slide rules were replaced by **electronic calculators**.
Slide rules were often used by engineers and draughtsmen.

soap *noun*

Soap is a fatty substance used for washing. It is a mixture of fat and chemicals called alkalis. Modern soaps often have perfumes or disinfectants added. Soap was first used in Mesopotamia about 5,000 years ago. It was made by boiling animal fat with wood ash and used as a medicine. In about 1200, vegetable oils began to be used instead of animal fat and the soap was used for washing.
Chemical detergents are sometimes used today instead of soap for washing clothes.

soda water *noun*

Soda water is a fizzy drink. It is made by adding a chemical called sodium bicarbonate to water. This produces carbon dioxide gas which gives soda water its fizz. Soda water is sold in bottles with screw caps to stop the gas from escaping. In 1772, **Joseph Priestley** was one of the first people to demonstrate how gas could be pumped into water.
Bottled lemonade is soda water with lemon flavouring added.

solar cell *noun*

A solar cell, or photovoltaic cell, is an electric **battery** that changes light **energy** into electrical energy. It contains a **semiconductor** in which electrons are made to move when light falls on them. Solar cells are used to provide **electricity** to operate the equipment of **satellites** in orbit. They also power some **electronic calculators**.
It is possible that, in the future, solar cells will provide power for electric cars.

solar furnace *noun*

A solar furnace is a device for collecting the rays of the Sun. Curved mirrors concentrate the rays. The rays are used to heat water and make steam. This drives a **steam turbine** which generates **electricity**. The first solar furnace to produce electric power was opened in California, United States of America in 1982.
Temperatures in a solar furnace can reach over 3000° Celsius.

solar motor *noun*

A solar motor is a small electric engine powered by light from the Sun collected by **solar cells**. So far, solar motors have been produced only for experiments. In 1981, a light **aircraft** powered by a solar motor flew from France to the United Kingdom. In 1986, a solar-powered car, the Sunrider, travelled from Greece to Portugal.
Panels of solar cells are used to collect light to power solar motors.

space shuttle *noun*

A space shuttle is a rocket-powered spacecraft. It is used to carry people, **satellites** and equipment from the Earth into space and back again. Two solid fuel rocket boosters and an outer fuel tank drop away after launch. The remaining section, the orbiter, continues its journey and lands back on Earth like a glider.
The first space shuttle was launched by the United States of America in 1981.

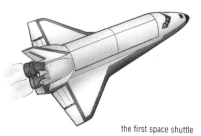

the first space shuttle

133

space station *noun*

A space station is a large spacecraft that is in permanent orbit. It has room for astronauts to live and work on board for long periods of time. **Space shuttles** can dock at the station's docking ports to deliver supplies and replacement crews. The first space station was Salyut 1, launched by the former Soviet Union in 1971. The American space station Skylab was occupied by three crews before breaking out of orbit in 1978.
Space station crews include scientists who carry out observations and experiments.

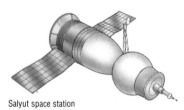

Salyut space station

space telescope *noun*

A space telescope is an **observatory** that is placed in orbit. It sends back television pictures of what it finds. The Hubble Space Telescope, built jointly by American and European space agencies, went into orbit in 1990. It was not a complete success because one of the **mirrors** was faulty, but it sent back useful information.
The Hubble Space Telescope was placed in orbit from a space shuttle.

spanner *noun*

A spanner is a **tool** for turning nuts and bolts. It has two jaws which fit the head of the nut. Box spanners are straight-sided tubes that fit over the nut. Adjustable spanners have a wheel that can be turned to alter the width of the gap between the jaws. Spanners were invented in Europe about 1550 and adjustable spanners in about 1700.
Mechanics keep a set of spanners to fit different sizes of nuts and bolts.

spare-part surgery *noun*

Spare-part surgery describes the replacement of a diseased body part by a healthy body part from another living person or from a dead body. Operations to carry out such replacements are called transplants. Kidneys, livers, hearts and lungs have all been successfully transplanted. The first completely successful kidney transplant was carried out in Boston, United States of America, in 1954.
The first heart transplant in the history of spare-part surgery took place in 1967.

spark plug *noun*

A spark plug is part of a petrol **internal combustion engine**. One plug is screwed into the top of each cylinder. The spark plug is connected to the car's electric circuit. The spark plug has two metal points separated by a gap. When **electricity** is fed to the plug, it jumps across the gap and makes a spark. This spark explodes the mixture of petrol and air in the cylinder.
Spark plugs have to be replaced when their points become worn.

spectacles *plural noun*

Spectacles are worn by people who have poor eyesight. They are frames that contain **lenses**. The lenses allow the wearer to see things more clearly. Spectacles are held onto the face by ear-pieces. The first spectacles were made in Italy about 1280. Single **magnifying glasses** had been used earlier.
Some people need to wear spectacles for reading.

hand-held folding spectacles, known as a lorgnette

speedometer *noun*
A speedometer is an instrument that is found on the dashboard of a **motor car**. It shows the car's speed. A cable joins the speedometer with the car's transmission shaft. A **gear** on the shaft makes a wire inside the cable turn, and this moves a needle on the dial of the speedometer.
The dial of a speedometer is often marked in both miles and kilometres per hour.

spinning and weaving ►page 136

spinning machine *noun*
A spinning machine is a device for spinning yarn or thread by twisting plant, animal or artificial fibres. The first spinning machine was called the spinning jenny. This hand-driven machine allowed up to eight threads to be spun at the same time. It was invented by a British weaver, James Hargreaves, in 1764. In 1779, Samuel Crompton invented an improved machine called the mule, which prevented the yarn breaking easily.
Richard Arkwright invented a water-powered spinning machine in 1771.

spinning wheel *noun*
A spinning wheel is a device for spinning yarn. The spinner turns a **wheel** which is joined by a belt to a spindle. Thread is spun as the spindle turns. Previously, thread was spun by pulling and twisting fibres from a hand-held distaff to a spindle. The spinning wheel was probably invented in India around 1000. It appeared in Europe around 1400.
Spinning wheels were used mainly by women working in their own homes.

spray gun *noun*
A spray gun is a device for producing a mist of liquid droplets. It forces liquid through a narrow opening in a nozzle. When the liquid reaches the air, it breaks up into droplets. Spray guns are used in car factories to apply paint to the bodies of the cars.
Small spray guns are often used to water indoor plants.

stage coach *noun*
A stage coach was a means of **public transport**. It was drawn by horses, and travelled by a regular timetable between cities. People could join or leave the coach at various points, or stages, on the journey. Stage coaches could not compete with express **trains**. They disappeared soon after the building of the **railways** in the 1830s.
The horses that pulled stage coaches were changed every few miles.

stained glass *noun*
Stained glass is **glass** that is coloured while being made. Pieces of stained glass are joined with others to make colourful windows. Stained glass is often seen in churches. It was probably first made in the Middle East.
By AD 500, simple stained glass was sometimes used in European churches.

stained glass window, Le Mans Cathedral, 1100s

stainless steel *noun*
Stainless steel is a metal. It is special steel containing nickel and chromium. It stands up to rusting and scratching. Stainless steel is often used for cutlery and kitchen equipment. It was invented in 1913 by a British steelmaker, Harold Brearley. The first stainless steel knives were made in 1914.
Stainless steel looks highly polished and like a mirror.

stave ► musical notation

spinning and weaving *noun*

Spinning and weaving describes the two processes involved in the making of cloth. Spinning prepares the fibre by twisting it and drawing it out into a long thread, or yarn. Weaving pulls all the fibres together, crossing them one over the other to make a length of cloth. The cloth can then be used to make items such as **clothing** and blankets.

The machines used for spinning and weaving have developed quickly since the Industrial Revolution.

early spindle

early loom

Spinning and weaving began about 10,000 y ago. Simple spindles were used for spinning yarn. The first looms were probably no more a pair of sticks that held the set of parallel th called the warp. By about 7000 BC, looms h horizontal rods to separate the threads.

Some modern looms can weave two or more kinds of cloth at the same time and at high speed. This small one can produce a huge range of colourful woven cloth with different patterns and textures.

Jacquard's automated loom, 1801

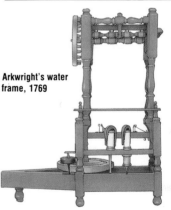

Arkwright's water frame, 1769

Medieval pedal-operated frame loom

Saxony spinning wheel, late 1400s

James Hargreaves' spinning jenny, 1764

knitting machine, invented by William Lee in 1589

steam car *noun*

A steam car was a **road vehicle**. It was used for transport before the **internal combustion engine** was invented. It had a heavy **steam engine**. The first road vehicle driven by steam was a three-wheeled **wagon** designed to pull heavy guns. It was invented by a French soldier, **Nicolas-Joseph Cugnot**, in 1769.

The American firm Stanley went on making steam cars until the 1920s.

Cugnot's steam car, used for pulling guns along

steam engine *noun*

A steam engine is a machine that uses heat **energy** to do work. It contains a **boiler** in which water is boiled to make steam. The steam is then used to move a piston in a cylinder. Steam engines were first used to pump water from mines. The first really efficient steam engine was designed by a Scottish engineer, **James Watt**, in the 1760s. It was an improved version of an engine invented by **Thomas Newcomen** in 1712.

Steam engines provided the power for the Industrial Revolution of the 1800s.

steam hammer *noun*

A steam hammer is a **machine** which is used in forging iron and steel. It is a heavy piece of metal called a tup. This is driven down onto an anvil by a steam-powered piston. The steam hammer was invented in 1839 by a Scottish engineer, James Nasmyth. Its first job was to forge the drive shaft of the steamship 'Great Britain'.

The steam hammer speeded up the production of iron and steel objects.

steam locomotive *noun*

A steam locomotive is a **vehicle** designed to push or pull **wagons** or carriages. Its driving **wheels** are powered by a **steam engine**. Some steam locomotives were built to travel on roads. These were sometimes called traction engines. Most steam locomotives were built specially for railway use. **Richard Trevithick**, a British engineer, built the first steam locomotive in 1804.

Steam locomotives were the railways' main source of power for about 150 years.

steam road-roller *noun*

A steam road-roller was a **vehicle** that was used to make a hard surface on roads. It was a steam traction engine with heavy **wheels** which acted as rollers. The rollers squeezed, or compressed, the road surface. Tools could be attached to break up or scrape a surface before renewing it. Steam road-rollers were first made by an English company, Aveling and Porter, in the 1860s.

Diesel road-rollers have taken the place of steam road-rollers.

steam turbine *noun*

A steam turbine is a **machine** for changing heat **energy** into mechanical energy. Steam is made in **boilers** and fed under pressure to turbine blades. These are metal blades with slots in them for the steam to pass through. The steam makes the blades turn. The first successful steam turbine was invented by a British engineer, Charles Parsons, in 1884.

Steam turbines are used in power stations to generate electricity.

steamboat *noun*

A steamboat is a **ship** powered by a **steam engine**. The first workable steamboat was invented in 1787 by the American John Fitch. The first steamboat to go into regular service was Robert Fulton's 'Clermont'. There are few steamboats left now. Modern ships are powered by oil engines.

The first steamboats had sails as well as engines in case the engines broke down.

Stephenson, George (1781–1848)

George Stephenson was born in Wylam, England. He became an engineer and built some of the first railway locomotives. His engine 'Locomotion' was used at the opening of the world's first public railway in 1825. Stephenson's 'Rocket' was another famous early locomotive. Stephenson helped to build many British railways. His son Robert was also a railway-builder and helped his father build the 'Rocket'.
George Stephenson never went to school, and taught himself to read and write.

stethoscope ► **medical invention**

stirrups *plural noun*
Stirrups are foot-rests used by horse-riders. They are loops of iron which hang by leather straps from the side of the **saddle**. Stirrups were invented in China in about AD 300.
Stirrups allowed cavalry soldiers to steady themselves in the saddle.

stocking frame ► **knitting machine**

stopwatch *noun*
A stopwatch is a kind of **watch** that is used to time events. In athletics, a stopwatch records the time taken by a runner in a race. The stopwatch starts counting time when the race begins. It stops when the winner passes the finishing line.
A modern stopwatch can measure time in hundredths of a second.

stove *noun*
A stove is an appliance for cooking food and sometimes also for heating. Some stoves use oil or coal as fuel. Others burn gas or electricity. Stoves can boil, fry, grill and bake food. The stove developed from the open kitchen fire. In the 1880s, gas stoves became available, and electric stoves were on sale by 1894. From 1915, thermostats were used to control the temperature.
Modern kitchen stoves have extra devices such as automatic timers and programmers.

street-cleaning machine *noun*
A street-cleaning machine is a **vehicle** that washes and sweeps city streets. It sprays the road surfaces with water. Then, rotating brushes sweep litter and dust into a storage bin. Street-cleaning machines usually work at night so that they do not disturb people or other traffic.
Street-cleaning machines move slowly when they are at work.

street lighting *noun*
Street lighting is **lighting** that is provided at night in towns and cities. The first street lights burned oil. The first street in the world to have lighting by gas was Pall Mall in London, in 1807. Each lamp had to be individually lit. Electric street lighting is switched on and off automatically by **time switches** or light-sensitive switches.
Mercury vapour lamps are often used for street lighting.

submarine *noun*

A submarine is a boat that can travel under water. It is fitted with buoyancy tanks. These can be filled with sea-water for diving, or emptied to bring a submerged submarine to the surface. Submarines are powered by diesel engines or nuclear reactors. The first submarine was built of wood and leather in 1620 by **Cornelis Drebbel**, a Dutch inventor living in England.

The first modern submarine was built in 1875 by an American, John P. Holland.

design for submarine by inventor Simon Lake, 1895

submersible *noun*

A submersible is a small craft that can travel under water. It usually has a crew of two, three or four. Submersibles are used by scientists to study deep sea wildlife. They are also used by engineers to examine oil rigs and other underwater structures. Some submersibles are fitted with tools which can be operated by remote control from inside the craft.

Like submarines, submersibles have tanks which are filled with water for diving.

sundial *noun*

A sundial is a **timekeeping** device. It is useful only during the day when the Sun is shining. The time is marked on a dial by the shadow of an arm or needle, called a **gnomon**, mounted at the centre. Sundials are sometimes found as ornaments in gardens and parks. The Ancient Egyptians used sundials as early as 1500 BC.

Travellers often carried portable sundials with them on long journeys.

supermarket *noun*

A supermarket is a large store that sells groceries and other household products. Shoppers choose the goods from the shelves and take them to a checkout. Here, the items are listed and the money to be paid is worked out automatically.

Supermarkets are convenient because you can buy what you need at just one store.

supersonic aircraft ▶ aircraft

suspension bridge *noun*

A suspension bridge is a **bridge** with a deck suspended from strong cables. Tall towers at each end of a suspension bridge support the cables. The cables are anchored at each end of the bridge behind the towers. New York's Brooklyn Bridge, built in 1883, and Zaire's Matadi Bridge are two well-known suspension bridges.

Suspension bridges are often built where there is a wide gap to be spanned.

Swan, Sir Joseph Wilson (1828–1914)

Sir Joseph Swan was born in Sunderland, England. He was trained as a chemist and made many inventions in the field of electrical engineering. In 1878, he invented the electric **light bulb** independently of his American rival, **Thomas Alva Edison**. Swan's and Edison's companies joined forces in 1883 to manufacture light bulbs.

Sir Joseph Wilson Swan invented a silk-like artificial fibre.

synthesizer *noun*

A synthesizer is an **electronic** musical instrument. The player works a keyboard to produce a large variety of sounds. These may copy conventional instruments. They may be pure electronic sounds, or include sound effects. The first synthesizer was made in the United States of America in 1953. Robert A. Moog invented an improved version in 1964.

Moog synthesizers are part of the equipment of many rock bands.

Talbot, William Henry Fox
(1780–1877)
William Henry Fox Talbot was an English mathematician and scientist who made important contributions to **photography**. He invented the negative-positive process of developing. For the first time, this enabled copies of photographs to be made. Fox Talbot also invented an enlarger and took the first photograph in electric light.
William Henry Fox Talbot's book, The Pencil of Nature, 1846, was the first in the world illustrated by photographs.

tank *noun*
A tank is an armoured fighting **vehicle**. It runs on caterpillar tracks. A tank can carry **arms** such as **machine guns**, **rockets**, flame-throwers or nuclear weapons. Tanks were invented by the British and first used in 1916, during the First World War. **Leonardo da Vinci** drew a tank in the 1400s.
Tanks can be used in rough country where wheeled vehicles would get into difficulties.

tanker *noun*
A tanker is a kind of **ship** designed to carry a liquid cargo. Tankers usually carry oil, but some also carry molasses, asphalt, wine or liquefied gas. The cargo space takes up about 60 per cent of the tanker's length. The space is divided into several large compartments. The first specially designed oil tanker was launched in Germany in 1886.
The largest tankers can carry up to 500,000 tonnes of cargo.

Tannoy ► **public address system**

tape recorder *noun*
A tape recorder is a device for **recording** sound and playing back the recordings. The sound is recorded as electric signals on plastic **magnetic tape**. A tape recorder using steel wire was invented in Denmark by Valdemar Poulsen in 1898. Plastic tape was first developed in 1935, and further improvements included stereophonic recording in 1958 and **Dolby sound** in 1966.
Tape recorders did not become popular until the tape cassette was invented in the 1960s.

telephone *noun*
The telephone is a form of **communicating**. It allows people to speak directly to each other. The vibrations of their voices are changed into electric signals. Then they are carried through a network of telephone lines. The telephone was invented in 1876 by **Alexander Graham Bell**, a Scotsman living in the United States of America.
Telephone conversations from one country to another are often beamed by satellite.

telephone answering machine *noun*
A telephone answering machine automatically answers **telephone** calls. It is a small **tape recorder** which is switched on by the ringing of a telephone. The machine plays a recorded message to the caller and then records the caller's own message on tape. When the owner of the machine returns, the messages can be played back.
Some businesses use telephone answering machines to deal with enquiries at night.

telephone callbox *noun*

A telephone callbox is a public **telephone**. It can be used by putting in money or a special card. Callboxes are found in the street, at airports and railway stations and in stores.
Telephone callboxes are sometimes called payphones.

telephone exchange ► automatic telephone exchange

telescope *noun*

A telescope is a device for studying objects in the night sky. Optical telescopes use **lenses** and **mirrors** to present an image to the viewer or to a **camera**. Radio telescopes pick up radio waves from distant stars. The first optical telescope was made in 1608 by **Hans Lipperschey**, a Dutch lens-maker.
Even a small, cheap telescope can give fascinating images of the night sky.

teletext *noun*

Teletext is a system of transmitting written information by broadcast **television**. The teletext signals are broadcast in 'spare' lines of the television signal. Viewers equipped with a decoder can select pages of teletext information and display it on their screens. Teletext services include news, sports results, weather forecasts and business information.
Teletext signals cannot be seen when a television set is operating normally.

television *noun*

Television is a form of **broadcasting**. It is a means of sending pictures and sound, changed into electric signals, over a distance. A British inventor, **John Logie Baird**, produced a **television** image in 1926. Modern television is based on the ideas of A.A. Campbell Swinton, a brilliant Scottish engineer, in 1911. At that time, technology was not yet advanced enough for his ideas to be put into practice.
Colour television was broadcast for the first time in 1953.

telex *noun*

Telex is a system of **communicating** by telegraph. It uses special typewriters called teleprinters, or teletype. Teleprinters communicate in a code. Pressing the keys of one teleprinter causes the other to print the appropriate character. The teleprinter was invented in 1897 by a British inventor, Frederick Creed.
Telex services began in the 1930s.

temperature scales *plural noun*

Temperature scales are means by which heat is measured. Temperature is measured in units called degrees. The first practical temperature scale was devised by a German scientist, **Gabriel Fahrenheit**. On the Fahrenheit scale, water freezes at 32 degrees and boils at 212 degrees. The Celsius scale of 100 degrees was devised by a Swedish scientist, **Anders Celsius**, in 1742.
Water freezes at 0 degrees Celsius and boils at 100 degrees Celsius.

Tesla, Nikola (1856–1943)

Nikola Tesla was a Serb who emigrated to the United States of America and became a scientist and electrical engineer. He developed ways of using alternating electric current and in 1888 invented the AC motor. Tesla also developed and improved other electrical devices and played a part in the early development of radio transmission.
Nikola Tesla built his own research laboratory, named after him, in New York.

theodolite *noun*
A theodolite is an instrument used in surveying. It allows angles and gradients to be measured. A modern theodolite is made up of a **telescope** fitted with a spirit level. It is mounted on a tripod so that it can move freely in any direction. The first theodolite was invented in 1571 by the Englishman Leonard Digges. A theodolite is sometimes called a transit.
Highway engineers can often be seen using a theodolite to survey roads.

Theodorus of Samos (c. 556 BC)
Theodorus was a sculptor who lived on the Ancient Greek island of Samos. He worked in metal. Theodorus invented the craft of hollow casting statues in bronze, an alloy of copper and tin. Hollow casting allowed sculptors to produce figures that were strong but light, and could be cast in life-like poses.
Theodorus of Samos lived in Samos at the same time as Pythagoras.

thermometer *noun*
A thermometer is an instrument for measuring temperature. Most thermometers are based on the principle that certain substances swell, or expand, when heated. A medical thermometer contains mercury inside a thin glass tube. As the mercury heats, it rises up the tube. A scale on the side of the tube indicates the temperature. The mercury thermometer was invented in 1714 by a German, **Gabriel Fahrenheit.**
Thermometers containing ethyl alcohol are used to measure very low temperatures.

Thermos flask ► vacuum flask

threshing machine *noun*
A threshing machine is a device for separating grains of wheat from the chaff. For thousands of years, this was a task done by hand with a flail. In 1786, a Scotsman, Andrew Meikle, invented the first threshing machine. It could be driven by horse, water or steam power. Today, threshing is done inside a **combine harvester**.
Before threshing machines were invented, threshing the harvest could take months.

time switch *noun*
A time switch is an electrical switch linked to a clock. It can be set to turn an electric current on and off at certain times. The movement of the clock mechanism makes or breaks contact at the preset times. Time switches are used in central heating systems, cookers, video recorders and many other devices around the house.
Time switches can turn your house lights on while you are out.

timekeeping ► page 144

tin can *noun*
A tin can is a container made of sheet steel with a thin covering of tin. It is used for preserving food. The food is sterilized to kill the bacteria which cause food to rot, and then sealed inside the can. The tin can was invented by the Englishman Peter Durand in 1810. Tin cans were first used on a large scale by two British manufacturers, John Hall and Bryan Donkin, in 1813.
Hall and Donkin supplied food in tin cans to the British Navy.

tin opener *noun*
A tin opener is a device for opening **tin cans**. When canned food first appeared, the cans had to be opened with a hammer and chisel. The first tin openers appeared around 1860.
Early tin openers had a blade which cut into the lid and levered it off.

timekeeping *noun*

Timekeeping is the recording of the passage of time. It is done on **clocks** and **watches** that can be mechanical or **electronic**. Early timekeeping relied on shadows cast by the Sun. These were measured by such devices as **sundials** and timesticks. **Water clocks**, **hourglasses** and **candle clocks** were other early timekeeping devices.

Modern quartz clocks are very accurate timekeeping devices.

Egyptian shadow clock, 2000 B

Prehistoric people probably told the time by looking at shadows cast by the Sun. Shadow clocks, or sundials, are the oldest known instruments for telling the time. They were developed more than 4,000 years ago.

The caesium atomic clock, invented in 1955, is the most accurate clock ever made. It would lose one second in 30,000 years.

balance-spring watch, late 1600s

Christiaan Huygens (1629–1659)

144

Egyptian water clock, 1400 BC

Water clocks were first used in Egypt in about 1400 BC.

This complicated water clock was built in 1088, by Su Sung of China. A water wheel worked bells, gongs and drums to mark the hours.

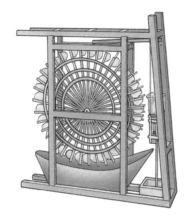

French coiled-spring watch of about 1540

The first practical pendulum clock was invented by Christiaan Huygens of Holland in 1657. He also designed a balance-spring watch in 1675. It was much more accurate than the earlier coiled-spring watches.

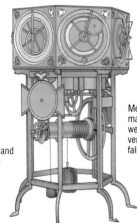

Mechanical clocks were first made in Europe by 1300. They were driven by a device called a verge escapement, worked by a falling weight.

Giovanni de Dondi's weight-driven clock, 1300s

toilet ► water closet

tool *noun*
A tool is a device for carrying out a certain task. The first tools were made in the Stone Age about two million years ago, probably in eastern Africa. They were stone axes, roughly shaped by chipping flints together. Smaller flakes of flint were used as cutting edges.
Stone Age people used their tool-making skills to make weapons for hunting.

toothbrush *noun*
A toothbrush is a device for cleaning the teeth. It has a plastic handle at one end and bristles, usually made of **nylon**, at the other. Toothbrushes have been in use since 1649, and toothpaste since 1660.
A toothbrush should be replaced frequently as the bristles become soft and worn.

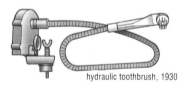
hydraulic toothbrush, 1930

toothed wheel ► gear

toothpaste tube *noun*
A toothpaste tube is an aluminium or plastic tube with a nozzle and a cap at one end.
Tubes began to replace jars of toothpaste in the United States of America in 1891.

torpedo (plural **torpedoes**) *noun*
A torpedo is a weapon used to sink enemy **ships**. It is made up of an explosive warhead, an engine and a tail with rudders and propellers. Some torpedoes carry nuclear warheads. The torpedo was invented by a British engineer, Robert Whitehead, in 1867.
Torpedoes can be fired by surface ships, but they are more often used in submarines.

trace harness ► harness

tractor *noun*
A tractor is a **vehicle** for use on farms. It can draw a variety of trailers and tools. Tractors have petrol or diesel engines. They have large rear wheels with thick tyres so that they do not get stuck in soft ground. The first petrol-engined tractor was built by the American Charter Engine Company in 1889.
Tractors do all the work about the farm that used to be done by horses.

traffic lights *plural noun*
Traffic lights are coloured light signals. They are placed at junctions and other places along roads to warn and guide drivers. They are fitted with red, green and amber **lenses**. Sensors in the road control the changing of the lights. The first traffic lights, worked by hand, were seen in New York City, United States of America, in 1914.
It is against the law for drivers to ignore traffic light signals.

train *noun*
A train is a line of carriages or wagons pulled or pushed by a locomotive along a **railway**. Trains may carry passengers or freight. Their locomotives are powered by steam, oil or electricity. The first experimental steam train ran on the Pen-y-Darren tramway in Wales, in 1804. It was built by the British engineer, **Richard Trevithick**.
Express trains are fast trains which run between major cities.

American train, 1832

tram *noun*
A tram is a passenger vehicle that runs on rails along city streets. It has an **electric motor** that takes its supply from overhead cables. In the United States of America, electric trams are called 'streetcars'. A German electrical engineer, Ernst von Siemens, built the first overhead-powered tram system in Berlin, Germany, in 1881.
Electric trams are a clean and efficient form of public transport in large cities.

transformer *noun*
A transformer is a device found in many electric circuits. It changes the voltage of an electric current passing through it by a process called electromagnetic induction. Transformers are found in many pieces of electrical equipment, such as **television** receivers. They are also found in the mains electricity supply network. The transformer was invented by an Englishman, **Michael Faraday**, in 1831.
The main parts of a transformer are two coils of wire and an iron core.

transistor *noun*
A transistor is an electronic device used to increase, or amplify, current in many types of electrical equipment. It is made of three pieces of **semiconductor** material which change the current passing through them. The transistor was invented in 1948 by three American scientists, John Bardeen, Walter Brattain and William Shockley.
Transistors are used in radio and television sets and many other domestic appliances.

traveller's cheque *noun*
A traveller's cheque is a form of money that can be used by travellers abroad. Hotels, restaurants and shops all accept traveller's cheques. The cheques can also be used to buy air, rail or sea travel. The first traveller's cheques were issued in 1866 by the British travel agent, Thomas Cook.
Thomas Cook called his traveller's cheques 'hotel coupons'.

treadmill *noun*
A treadmill is a device for using people or animals to power a machine. It is a large, open **wheel** inside which there are steps. As the person or animal walks on the steps, the wheel turns. The Ancient Romans used slaves in treadmills to provide power for **cranes**. In Europe, dogs were placed in treadmills to turn the spit on which meat was cooked.
Treadmills were used in British prisons until about 100 years ago.

Trevithick, Richard (1771–1833)
Richard Trevithick was a British engineer who built one of the first **steam locomotives**. He built a model first, and then a full-scale version. In 1808, he demonstrated one of his locomotives in London. Then he went abroad to use his steam engines in silver mines in Peru. When he came back, others had taken up his ideas and improved on them.
Richard Trevithick's first steam locomotive was called the 'Puffing Devil'.

tricycle *noun*
A tricycle is a three-wheeled **vehicle** powered by the rider. It is similar to a **bicycle**. There are pedals for the rider's feet and a pair of handlebars for steering. As with a bicycle, the front wheel is the steering wheel. Tricycles became popular in the 1870s and 1880s, when bicycles were heavy and hard to ride.
The tricycle rickshaw is widely used in Asia.

trolley bus *noun*
A trolley bus is an electrically-powered passenger **road vehicle**. It takes power from overhead cables in the same way as a **tram**, but a trolley bus does not run on rails. The first ones were adapted by the German Siemens company from electric trams in about 1900.
Trolley buses cause no air pollution.

turbine *noun*
A turbine is a kind of **engine**. It uses a stream of flowing gas or liquid to turn a shaft and drive machinery. The water turbine was developed in the 1820s by the French engineer Benoit Fourneyron. The steam turbine was invented by Charles Parsons, a British engineer, in 1884. Modern **gas turbines** were invented in about 1905.
In a turbine, the force of gas or liquid passing the blades makes the shaft turn.

typesetting machine *noun*
A typesetting machine is a device that puts together, or composes, lines of type for **books** and newspapers. The first successful machine was invented in 1884 by a German watchmaker, Ottmar Mergenthaler. His machine was called the **Linotype**. It cast lines of type out of lead. Today's typesetting machines are programmed by **computers**.
The invention of typesetting machines made books and newspapers cheaper.

typewriter *noun*
A typewriter is a machine for producing printed material. The user operates a keyboard which causes the right characters to be printed on paper. Some typewriters have electric or electronic parts. Between 1714 and 1874, many people tried to make a typewriter. The final winner was Christopher Sholes of Milwaukee, United States of America. His machine, the Remington, appeared in 1874.
Typewriters with computer drives are called word processors.

ultrasonic scanner *noun*
An ultrasonic scanner is a kind of detecting device. It sends out very high sound frequencies called ultrasound. The frequencies are reflected back from an object, and can be used to build up a picture on a screen. Ultrasonic scanners are used in hospitals to check on the health of unborn babies. They are also used in laboratories to detect faults in metal. In 1952, the American doctor, Robert Lee Wild, was the first to use ultrasound for medical purposes.
Ultrasonic scanners are often used instead of X-ray machines because they are safer.

ultraviolet lamp *noun*
An ultraviolet lamp is an electric **lamp** that gives off ultraviolet light. Ultraviolet light cannot be seen. The Sun gives out ultraviolet rays. Some people use ultraviolet lamps to give them an artificial suntan. However, too much exposure to ultraviolet light can be dangerous.
Small ultraviolet lamps are sometimes used to check documents for forged signatures.

umbrella *noun*
An umbrella is a device for protecting the user against rain or strong sun. It is usually circular, and is mounted on a long handle. The Ancient Chinese were using umbrellas with bamboo frames by 1100 BC. Umbrellas were also used in Ancient Egypt as a status symbol. The modern, folding umbrella, with steel ribs and a silk or cotton covering, dates from the 1800s.
People use umbrellas as much for fashion as for protection from the weather.

148

underground railway *noun*

An underground railway is a city **railway** system with tracks that are mostly or entirely underground. Underground trains are powered by **electric motors**. The first underground railway was built in London, England, in 1863. It is still in use. More than 30 cities throughout the world have underground railway systems.

Underground railways allow thousands of people to make fast journeys to and from work each day.

universal joint *noun*

A universal joint is a device that is used to change the direction of a rotating shaft. It is used in cars to change the rotation of the drive shaft to that of the driving axle. The universal joint was invented in 1676 by the British scientist **Robert Hooke**. He used it in his astronomical instruments. The universal joint found its real value in the age of the **motor car**.

The two shafts connected in a universal joint can turn around each other in any direction.

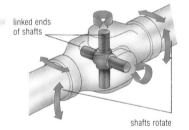

linked ends of shafts

shafts rotate

vacuum cleaner *noun*

A vacuum cleaner is an electrical appliance. It contains a fan, powered by an **electric motor**. This sucks up dust. The dust is collected in a paper bag that can be thrown away and replaced. The vacuum cleaner was invented in 1901 by a British engineer, Herbert Booth.

In 1908, an American manufacturer, William Hoover, marketed the 'upright' vacuum cleaner especially for carpets.

vacuum flask *noun*

A vacuum flask is a container that keeps hot liquids hot and cold liquids cold. It is a bottle made of two layers of thin glass, separated by a vacuum. The glass is given a mirror finish. This and the vacuum prevent heat from passing between the inside and outside of the flask. The vacuum flask was invented in 1892 by a Scottish scientist, James Dewar.

Vacuum flasks, with the trade name Thermos, first went on sale in 1925.

inner vacuum flask

vehicle *noun*

A vehicle is any wheeled means of transport used on land. The history of vehicles began around 3000 BC in Mesopotamia, where **wheels** were fitted for the first time to a cart.

The first vehicles were drawn by oxen.

velocipede *noun*

A velocipede was an early version of the **bicycle**. The pedals were fitted to the axle of the front wheel, which was slightly larger than the rear wheel. The velocipede had wooden wheels and thick iron tyres. Velocipedes were invented by two French brothers, Pierre and Ernest Michause, in 1865. Velocipedes were very popular in France, Britain and the United States of America.

Velocipedes were very uncomfortable to ride and became known as 'boneshakers'.

vending machine *noun*

A vending machine is an automatic selling device. It delivers chocolate, drinks or other goods when it is operated by coins. Sensors inside the machine check that the right coins have been put into the machine. The Ancient Greek scientist **Hero of Alexandria** invented a water-vending machine in about AD 60. The first modern vending machine sold **chewing gum** at New York City railway stations in 1888.

Many schools have vending machines.

video camera *noun*

A video camera is a device that takes and **records** a television picture. Inside a video camera, an electron gun scans an image formed by the camera's **lens**. Different parts of the image produce different electric voltages, and these changes in voltage make up the video signal.

A small video camera that records onto video cassettes is called a camcorder.

video cassette *noun*

A video cassette is a plastic case containing a length of videotape. It is used to **record** and play back television images and sound, that are stored on the tape in the form of electronic signals. The modern form of video recording was developed in 1956 by the American Ampex Corporation. The first video cassette recorders were made in 1969 by Sony in Japan.

Video cassettes can be used to record programmes to be watched later.

video game *noun*

A video game is an **electronic** game that is played on a **visual display unit**. The player or players test their reactions to the features stored in the game program. A device called a joystick is often used by the players to take part in the game. The display on the screen features exciting computer graphics and flashing lights.

Manufacturers of video games are always trying to make them more exciting.

video recorder *noun*

A video recorder is an **electronic** device. It **records** broadcast television programmes on videotape. It collects the broadcast signals and stores them on the tape. A video recorder contains a timer that allows recordings to be planned in advance. Video recorders also play back videotapes through a television set.

The first successful video recorder was made in the USA in 1956 by Ampex.

Vinci, Leonardo da ► **Leonardo da Vinci**

visual display unit *noun*
A visual display unit, or VDU, is the screen on which **computer** information is displayed. **Electronic** signals from the computer's inputs and programs are changed into characters or graphics. These may appear on the VDU in colour or black and white. A VDU is sometimes called a 'monitor'.
Word processors have a VDU so that the user can see what has been typed.

Volta, Alessandro (1745–1827)
Alessandro Volta was an Italian scientist who specialized in the study of electricity. He made the first cell which produced electricity by chemical reaction. This discovery led to the electric batteries that are used today in torches and other small devices.
Alessandro Volta's name is remembered today when people speak of 'volts' as units of electricity.

voltaic pile *noun*
A voltaic pile was the first electric cell invented by Alessandro Volta. In 1800, he built it by placing pieces of zinc and copper on top of each other, separated by cloth soaked in salt. Reaction between the metals and the salt produced an electric current. Today's **batteries** work in a similar way.
The voltaic pile changes chemical energy into electrical energy.

VTOL aircraft *noun*
A VTOL aircraft is a fixed-wing **aeroplane** that can take off and land without using a runway. The letters VTOL stand for vertical take-off and landing. The aircraft is fitted with jets that can be pointed downwards for take-off or backwards for forward flight. The first successful VTOL aircraft was the P1127. This was designed and built in Britain in 1960 by Sir Sidney Camm.
The Harrier VTOL aircraft is sometimes called a 'jump jet'.

wagon *noun*
A wagon is a four-wheeled **vehicle**. Wagons were able to carry heavy loads because the weight of the load was shared between the two **axles**. Wagons were developed by the Sumerians in about 3000 BC. The people of Kocs in Hungary were expert wagon-builders. They lent the name of their village to one type of wagon, the coach.
When the railways came, the wagon was adopted as the pattern for rail vehicles.

Walkman ► **personal stereo**

wallpaper *noun*
Wallpaper is **paper** used to decorate the inside walls of buildings. It is supplied in long rolls and pasted to the wall surface to make a continuous pattern. Wallpaper was invented in China. It appeared in Europe in about 1481. It was made by hand in small sheets. Rolls of machine-made paper were sold from about 1800.
Wallpapers for kitchens and bathrooms are often made of vinyl and are washable.

washing machine *noun*
A washing machine is an appliance for washing, rinsing and drying laundry. A modern washing machine has an **electric motor** and takes water directly from the mains supply. One of a number of washing programmes can be chosen. Hand-operated washing machines appeared in the 1850s. The first modern machine was developed in 1910 by an American, Alva J. Fisher.
A washing machine switches itself off when it has completed its programme.

watch *noun*

A watch is a small **timekeeping** device. It is worn either on the wrist or attached to clothing. Until recently, all watches had clockwork motors. **Electronic** watches contain a vibrating quartz crystal that keeps accurate time. Watches show the time either by the position of hands on a dial or by a **digital** display. Mechanical watches were invented in Germany in about 1500.
Electronic watches are powered by a tiny battery that lasts for about one year.

water clock *noun*

A water clock is a **timekeeping** device. It is a bowl with a hole in the base. As water trickles through the hole, marks on the inside of the bowl show the passing of time. Water clocks were in use by about 1415 BC. The Ancient Egyptians used water clocks to keep the time at night.
The Ancient Greeks copied the idea of the water clock and improved on it by adding a dial and an hour hand.

water closet *noun*

A water closet is a device for flushing away wastes from the human body. It has a cistern full of water which is released when a lever or chain is pulled. The water flushes from the lavatory pan into the sewers. An English nobleman, Sir John Harington, drew a water closet in 1589. It was not until 1778 that another Englishman, **Joseph Bramah**, made the first working example.
The invention of the water closet marked an important step forward in hygiene.

Bramah's water closet, 1778

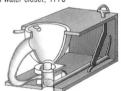

water colour pigment cake *noun*

Water colour pigment cake is a block of colours, or pigments, mixed with gum arabic from the acacia tree. An artist uses a brush to mix the colour with water before putting it onto paper. The Chinese painted in water colours from about AD 900. They used pigment cake made from such materials as lampblack and animal skins.
The gum in water colour pigment cake helps the colour to stick to the paper.

water filtration system *noun*

A water filtration system is a series of processes which clean water. It is part of a water pumping station. The water takes about eight hours to pass through tanks. Here, the water seeps through filters and chemicals are added to it. The first water filtration system, using sand as a filter, was built in London in 1827.
Water filtration systems aid health by removing harmful bacteria from drinking water.

water mill *noun*

A water mill is a device for grinding wheat into flour. It makes use of the energy of flowing water to drive a waterwheel. The waterwheel's shaft is connected through **gears** to grindstones. The water mill was probably invented by the Romans around 100 BC. Later, water mills were used to operate sawmills and in cloth manufacture.
The water mill was the first example of the use of water power.

water transport ▶ page 154

watermark *noun*
A watermark is a design applied to **paper** when it is made. It can be seen by holding the paper up to the light. The design often shows the name or trade mark of the maker of the paper. **Postage stamps**, **banknotes** and other documents usually carry a watermark to prevent forgery.
Papermakers in Italy began to use watermarks in about AD 1250.

waterproof *adjective*
Waterproof describes any material that does not allow water to seep through. Rubber and **plastics** are used to waterproof materials.
The first waterproof material was invented in 1823 by a Scottish chemist, Charles Macintosh.

water turbine ▶ turbine

waterwheel ▶ water mill

Watson-Watt, Sir Robert (1892–1973)
Sir Robert Watson-Watt was a Scottish scientist who invented **radar**. In 1919, he began his experiments in using radio waves to find directions. By 1935, he had demonstrated a system of tracing the position and distance of enemy aircraft by radar. He set up a network of secret radar stations for the British government.
Sir Robert Watson-Watt's radar allowed Britain to spot enemy bombers.

Watt, James (1736–1879)
James Watt was a Scottish mechanical engineer. He made improvements to the **steam engine** invented by Thomas Newcomen. He was not the inventor of the steam engine, but did play an important part in its development. With Matthew Boulton, he made many hundreds of engines. These were used as pumping engines in mines.
The modern unit of power, the watt, is named after James Watt.

weaving ▶ spinning and weaving

weighing machine *noun*
A weighing machine is a device for measuring weight. Many different kinds of weighing machine have been invented. The oldest is the simple balance, which was in use over 5,000 years ago in Mesopotamia. Modern weighing machines show the weight of goods as a liquid crystal display and are controlled by **microprocessors**.
Simple weighing machines are still used by market traders in many parts of the world.

weights and measures *plural noun*
Weights and measures are measurements to show the size and weight of things. Different systems have been used in different parts of the world which are still sometimes used for everyday things. But all scientists today use a system called SI units. These are based on the **metric system** introduced in France in 1799. The SI was accepted internationally in 1960.
SI stands for Système Internationale.

Westinghouse, George (1846–1914)
George Westinghouse was an American engineer who invented the **air brake** for railway trains. This allowed all the brakes on a train to be controlled by the driver. It meant that trains could travel safely at higher speeds.
George Westinghouse developed an electric signalling system for the railways.

water transport *noun*

Water transport is the carrying of goods or people by water. Before **bridges** began to be built, boats were the only means of crossing rivers or lakes. Before the age of the **aeroplane**, **ships** were the only way seas and oceans could be crossed. In prehistoric times, water transport was simply floating logs or driftwood. The first boats were logs hollowed out to make **canoes**. The most advanced ships today are nuclear-powered. *Water transport has been used for thousands of years.*

dugout canoe, 8000 BC

modern hydrofoil, first invented by Enrico Forlanini in 1906

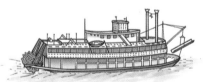

Mississippi sternwheeler paddle boat, 1820

Chinese junk, 1400s

coracle, 6000 BC

Egyptian wooden cargo ship, 2500 BC

Viking longship, AD 1000

Greek trireme, 400 BC

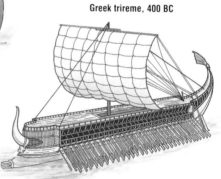

wheel ► page 157

wheelbarrow *noun*
A wheelbarrow is a small **vehicle** with one
wheel and two handles. It is used for moving
small quantities of earth or other material.
Because it has only one wheel, it is easy to
steer and manoeuvre. The wheelbarrow was
invented in China about 100 BC and was
used to carry goods and people.
The wheelbarrow's design has changed
very little since it was invented.

Whitney, Eli (1765–1825)
Eli Whitney was an American lawyer who
invented the cotton gin. This was a machine
for separating cotton fibres from the seeds
round which they grow. Before, the job had
been done by hand. The invention of the gin
led to a huge increase in cotton-growing in
the southern United States of America. Later,
Eli Whitney became a successful
manufacturer of rifles.
Eli Whitney's invention of the cotton gin led
to great prosperity for the cotton growers.

wind gauge ► anemometer

windmill *noun*
A windmill is a **machine** for grinding wheat
into flour. It has sails made of wood which
are driven round by wind power. They in turn
drive a shaft, which is connected to the
millstones. The first windmills were probably
built in central Asia, where winds are strong
and long-lasting. Windmills appeared in
Europe in about the 1200s. They remained
an important means of grinding wheat for
over 700 years.
Windmills were also used in some places as
a source of energy for irrigation.

windscreen wipers *plural noun*
Windscreen wipers clear rain or mist off a
car's windscreen. They consist of rubber
blades mounted on metal arms.
The first mechanical windscreen wipers
appeared in 1916 in the USA.

wind turbine *noun*
A wind turbine is a device for making, or
generating, **electricity** from wind power. It
has blades similar to the blades of an aircraft
propeller. These turn in the wind and their
energy of movement is changed into
electrical energy. Large numbers of wind
turbines are often built together on wind
farms.
Wind turbines can provide useful energy for
small communities far away from public
electricity supplies.

wireless ► radio

word processor *noun*
A word processor is a kind of **computer**. It
creates, edits, prints and stores text. A word
processor's functions are controlled by a
microprocessor. The text is typed on a
keyboard similar to the keyboard of a
typewriter, and appears on a **visual display
unit**. It can be changed or corrected until the
user is satisfied. Then the text is printed on
paper and stored on a **floppy disk**.
It is easier to correct mistakes on a word
processor than on a typewriter.

Wright, Orville (1871–1948) **and Wilbur**
(1867–1912)
Orville and Wilbur Wright were two American
brothers who built and flew the first powered
aircraft. Orville made the first **flight**, lasting
12 seconds, on 17 December 1903. Soon,
the brothers were making longer flights, and
in 1905 they set up an aircraft company.
Wilbur Wright died in 1912 at the age of 45,
and Orville sold the Wright Company in
1915.
The Wright brothers were bicycle makers
before they became interested in flying.

wristwatch ► watch

writing ► page 158

wheel *noun*

The wheel was first invented about 3500 BC for making pottery. About 300 years later it was adapted for transport. The first wheels were made out of solid pieces of wood mounted on an axle. Gradually, wheels became lighter, and spokes were introduced. *The wheel gave human beings greater freedom to explore and use their environment.*

Assyrian spoke-wheeled chariot, c. 860 BC

Spoked wheels were being made by about 2000 BC. They even had metal rims to stop them wearing out.

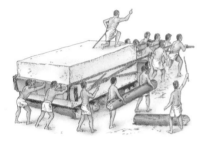

Before the invention of the wheel, people moved heavy loads on rollers made from logs.

pulley for lifting heavy weights, c. 3000 BC

The Sumerians invented the wheel about 5,000 years ago. They used wheels to make pottery and also fitted them to carts. Their wheels were solid and made from tree trunks.

Roman water mill for grinding wheat

Wheels have many other uses besides moving vehicles along. In the form of pulleys and gears, wheels have been used to drive many kinds of machine since early times.

writing *noun*

Writing is the use of symbols or characters to communicate with other people. The people of Mesopotamia developed a form of writing about 5,000 years ago. It was called cuneiform and was made up of wedge-shaped marks. The **alphabet** used in most parts of the world today was invented in Phoenicia about 3,000 years ago. It was later copied and adapted by the Ancient Greeks and Romans.

In Mesopotamia, the first writing was done on clay tablets using pointed sticks.

Sumerian pictographic writing

Writing was invented by the Sumerians in about 3500 BC. They made marks in soft clay with a reed stylus.

means	3000 BC	2000 BC	700 BC	500 BC
	◇	⋈	𒄑	𒀀
	✳	⬗	▸⊢	▸⊢
	⋚	⋜	⋆	⋆
	⟁	⟊	𒊹	⋇
	⇨	⇨	𒂗	𒂗
	⍀	⋇	𒅖	𒁹

development of cuneiform writing

In about 3000 BC, cuneiform writing was introduced in Persia, Syria and Babylon.

The Egyptians developed hieroglyphics in about 3000 BC.

𓂧𐤟 𐤟 𐤟 𐤟 𐤟 𐤟 𐤟 𐤟 𐤟 𐤟 𐤟 𐤟 𐤟

The first true alphabet appeared in about 1300 BC at Ugarit in Syria. Each of the 32 letters stood for a single sound.

ΑΒΓΔΕ ΖΗΘΙ ΚΛΜΝΞΟΠ ΡΣΤΥ

A Ͽ ϶Ⅎ ⸲Ⅎ⊙Ⅰ ⋊⌐⋎⋎⋈ ⇑ⱮQ4ϟⱵ∨

ABCDEFG H IJKLMN OP QRSTUVW

The Greek alphabet developed from the Ugarit alphabet in about 1000 BC. The Roman alphabet used in the West today developed from the Greek in about 400 BC.

1. Sumerian reed stylus
2. Egyptian hollow reed pen
3. Chinese writing brush
4. quill pen
5. dip pen
6. fountain pen
7. Biro ballpoint pen

3.

4.

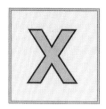

xerographic copying machine ▶
photocopier

X-rays   *plural noun*
X-rays are invisible waves of electromagnetic
radiation. Their wavelength is much shorter
than that of visible light. X-rays can travel
through some materials such as animal skin
and flesh. They are valuable in the treatment
of disease as they allow doctors to see
inside a human body. X-rays were
discovered in 1895 by a German scientist,
Wilhelm Röntgen.
*X-rays are used in industry to find faults in
the internal parts of machinery.*

xylophone   *noun*
A xylophone is a musical instrument. It is a
set of wooden bars of different lengths. The
bars vibrate and produce different notes
when struck by hammers. The xylophone is
part of the percussion section of an
orchestra. It is a very ancient instrument that
was probably invented in the Far East.
*The shorter bars of the xylophone produce
the higher-pitched notes.*

African log xylophone

yacht   *noun*
A yacht is a small boat used for pleasure.
It may have an **engine** or sails. Some yachts
are designed and built specially for racing.
Others are for cruising, and are fitted with
galleys, beds and other furniture. The yacht
was invented by the Dutch in about 1660.
The first known yacht race was held in 1662
between a Dutch yacht and one owned by
King Charles II of England.
*The Fastnet Race is an annual race in the
Atlantic between ocean-going yachts.*

Yale, Linus (1821–1868)
Linus Yale was the American inventor of the
Yale cylinder lock. He made the first one in
1848, but improvements were made 15
years later by his son, also called Linus.
The Yale lock could be mass-produced and
therefore sold cheaply.
*Linus Yale was a professional lock-maker
employed by American banks.*

Yale lock   *noun*
A Yale lock is a cylinder lock that contains a
number of pins on springs. The correct key
moves these pins aside and allows the lock
to be opened. The Yale lock was invented by
Linus Yale in 1848. He copied an idea that
the Ancient Egyptians used in their locks
about 4,000 years ago.
*To open a Yale lock, the pins in the cylinder
must line up with the notches on the key.*

Zeppelin ▶ **airship**

zip code ▶ **postcode**

zip fastener   *noun*
A zip fastener is a means of fastening
clothes. It is made up of two strips of metal
or plastic teeth that lock together. These can
be joined or undone by a sliding clip. The zip
fastener was invented in 1893 by an
American, Whitcomb Judson, as a fastening
for boots. It was introduced for clothes in the
1920s.
One of the earliest uses for the zip-fastener
was to fasten flying suits.

zoom lens   *noun*
A zoom lens is a **lens** in a movie or
television **camera**. It is made up of a number
of separate lenses which can be moved in
relation to each other. This makes the
camera appear to move closer to or further
away from an object, when in fact it does not
move at all.
A zoom lens is often used on television to
pick out one face in a crowd.